AF511885

Hinduism and its Development

Andhra University Philosophical Studies

Andhra University Philosophical Studies contain comprehensive works oriented to the traditions of Socrates and Sankara. With the motto, 'Global Understanding with Vedāntic Spirit' initiated by S. Radhakrishnan at Andhra University these volumes reflect ethics, social ideals and cultural values, embodied both in secular society and religious thought. Apart from brief texts on the Buddha and Sankara, volumes on Saints and Gurus, Social Relevance of Philosophy and Philosophical Teaching have been released. Volumes published under the series are:

1. Life and Teachings of Ādi Śaṅkarācārya; by P. George Victor (ISBN 81-246-0194-1)
2. Saints and Gurus: Perspectives on Spiritual and Social Renaissance in Contemporary India; edited by P. George Victor and S.D.A. Joga Rao (ISBN 81-246-0203-4)
3. Social Relevance of Philosophy: Essays on Applied Philosophy; edited by P. George Victor (ISBN 81-246-0204-2)
4. Teaching Philosophy in the Twenty-First Century; edited by P. George Victor (ISBN 81-246-0205-0)
5. Studies in Vedānta: Essays in Honour of Professor S.S. Rama Rao Pappu; edited by P. George Victor and V.V.S. Saibaba (ISBN 81-246-0350-2)
6. Discourses in Buddhist Classics; by V.V.S. Saibaba (ISBN 81-246-0360-X)
7. Hinduism and its Development; by K. Satchidananda Murty (ISBN 81-246-0383-9)
8. Evolution of Indian Philosophy; by K. Satchidananda Murty (ISBN 81-246-0393-6)

Andhra University Philosophical Studies, no. 7

Hinduism and its Development

by

K. Satchidananda Murty

D.K. Printworld (P) Ltd.
New Delhi

Cataloging in Publication Data — DK
[Courtesy: D.K. Agencies (P) Ltd. <docinfo@dkagencies.com>]

Satchidananda Murty, K. (Kotta), 1924-
Hinduism and its development / by K. Satchidananda Murty. — 2nd rev. ed.
p. 23 cm. — (Andhra University philosophical studies ; no. 7)
Includes bibliographical references (p.)
Includes index.
ISBN 8124603839 (hardbound)
ISBN 8124603847 (paperback)

1. Hinduism — History. I. Title. II. Series: Andhra University philosophical studies ; no. 7.

DDC 294.509 22

ISBN 81-246-0383-9 (hardbound)
ISBN 81-246-0384-7 (paperback)
Part I and II first appeared in 1947 as "Hinduism & its Development."
Part III first appeared in 1985 as "The Advaitic Notion."
Second revised edition published in 2007
© K. Satchidananda Murty

All rights reserved. No part of this publication may be reproduced or transmitted, except brief quotations, in any form or by any means, electronic or mechanical, including photocopying, recording, or any information storage or retrieval system, without prior written permission of the copyright holder, indicated above, and the publishers.

Published & printed by:
D.K. Printworld (P) Ltd.
Regd. Office: 'Sri Kunj', F-52, Bali Nagar
New Delhi-110 015
Phones: (011) 2545-3975; 2546-6019; *Fax*: (011) 2546-5926
E-mail: dkprintworld@vsnl.net
Website: www.dkprintworld.com

Preface to the First Edition

I

HINDUISM is too vast to be summed up in — short speeches, mainly intended for graduate and under-graduate students of a college. The omissions, which are noticeable, by any careful reader, have been inevitably deliberate.

Without being detrimental to individual views and ideals, Hinduism has built up a unity of spirit, which has survived the ravages of time. A recapture of this spirit, so unique to our religion and culture, is the essential need of these times of strife and tension. I shall be delighted if this brochure could attract the attention of some of our young men and women in the colleges towards that ideal.

II

Vācaspati expounded a number of philosophical systems as if he were a follower of each. . . .Following his example, I have sympathetically explained some of the ideas of Advaita Vedānta — relying only on classical sources, refraining from criticism or comparison — Awareness of consciousness, falsity of the world, the great Upaniṣadic Sentences and *Brahman*-knowledge in that order. This work sets forth the traditional stand point that only the great sentences of the *Upaniṣad*s could be the source of *Brahman*-knowledge and nothing else, clarifies that contemporary science cannot demolish any type of Eastern wisdom, and argues that Vedāntic sociology, social organization or action ought to conform to Vedāntic metaphysics.

With all his vast knowledge Nārada admitted: "I am only like a knower of words, not a knower of the self."[1] And when Asvala, the *hota* of king Janaka of Videha asked whether he was *brahmaniṣṭa*, the wisest among brāhmins, Yājñavalkya replied: "We bow to the *brahmaniṣṭa* while we just wish to have cows."[2]

The great Ibn Sina at one stage wrote that he did not know what he was and what he wished to become; and in our time Gabriel Marcel once exclaimed that he did not know what he believed. It is difficult for lesser men to have a firm awareness (*dṛḍa-bodha*) or clear assured conviction regarding transcendental truth.

III

"Therefore, a knower of *Brahman* ought to desire to live as a child:" *tasmad Brahmanah pandityam nirvidya balyena tishtaset.*[3] The *Muṇḍaka Upaniṣad* (1.2.11) states only those who practise *tapas* and *śraddhā* become tranquil-knower: *santo vidvamsah.* As Śrī Śaṅkara Bhāgavatpada explained, for the self-controlled (*praśānta*) the Supreme Self is immediately present as self: *jivatmanah prasantasya paramātma samahitah.*[4]

K. Satchidananda Murty

---

1. *Chāndogya Upaniṣad*, 7.1.1-3.
2. *Bṛhadāraṇyaka Upaniṣad*, 3.1.2.
3. *Ibid.*, 3.5.1.
4. *Gītā-bhāṣya*, 6.7.

Preface to the Second Edition

MAHAMAHOPADHYAYA K. Satchidananda Murty is the most thought-provoking philosopher of the twentieth century India, whose books on Indian philosophy, culture, religion — particularly Vedānta — contain an instructive and penetrating analysis, and fill the gaps that were left by famous writers, insisting on the relevance and the forgotten dimension of philosophical learning in India. This work of Professor K. Satchidananda Murty contains three parts.

I

In the first part, probably influenced by the Second World War, Professor Murty points out his spiritual vision of "global outlook" as the solution for everyday problems; thus the first section begins. In the second section, he proposed the spiritual vision of life to satisfy the needs of man rather than the religious rituals and dogmatic beliefs. The third section on Vedānta contains the metaphysical doctrines of the Upaniṣads, bringing their significance for mankind. In the fourth section he asserts that the religious practice is nothing but the assertive life of righteousness. The racial element in the evolution of caste-system in India has also been theorized apart from a discussion on the Hindu view of life.

The second part of this work, which is a continuity of the first part, constitutes twelve sections, tracing the evolution of Hinduism. An attempt is made to narrate the historical, doctrinal, and logical evolution of Hinduism from the times of Indus Valley civilization to the modern age of Vivekānanda and Mahatma Gandhi by interpreting the influence of the Moguls and the British on Indian life. The Greek connection, the conglomeration of Buddhism and Islam with Indian spirit have found a place.

The third part of this work, which was written in 1985 and entitled the *Vedāntic Vision,* was divided into five sections and stands for what Professor Murty stood and strived as a teacher of philosophy. He asserts that as the Vedāntic teaching establishes that everyone's self is *Brahman* and the Vedic scriptures have spoken that the self of all is non-dual, the "Advaitic Vision" (*advaita buddhi*) is possible through the study of the scriptures. As Śaṅkara and the later Vedānta followers have asserted the *mithyātva* of the world, which lacks absolute permanence, Professor Murty argues that the passion for the world and wealth is absolutely a futile exercise.

Professor Murty remarks that the transcendental knowledge of Vedānta does not need any support from the modern scientific theories. The metaphysical teachings of Advaita Vedānta imply in the social sphere — equanimity towards all by seeking their welfare, as Śaṅkarācārya comments that the true self is devoid of distinctions like brāhmin, kṣatriya, etc. Being grounded in Hindu tradition, trained in Sanskrit language and endowed with profound scholarship of Vedānta, Professor Murty's commentary on the social implications of Vedāntic metaphysics is significant.

II

The first and second parts of this work were actually a series of "lectures delivered under the religious education scheme of the S.V. College, Tirupati" on the invitation of Sir Gopati

Narayanaswamy Chetti, President of the College Committee of the Tirumala Tirupati Devasthanam. Subsequently published in 1947 as *Hinduism and its Development* by Sundara Ram & Sons, Tenali in Andhra Pradesh, this brochure was dedicated to Dr. Sir Ramalinga Reddi of Cattamanchi, the then Vice-Chancellor of Andhra University, whom Professor K. Satchidananda Murty considers "the symbol of cultural synthesis and intellectual integrity."

The third part of this work is the address delivered in Tenali town during the celebration of the Silver Jubilee of *Śrī Śaṅkara Kṛpā*, a Telugu journal "in the presence of H.H. Jagadguru Śrī Bhārati Tīrtha Swami of Śṛṅgerī Śāradā Pīṭha on September 16, 1985." Dedicated with profound reverence to H.H. Paramahaṁsa Parivrājakācārya Jagadguru Śrī Abhinava Vidyātīrtha Mahāsvāmī of Śṛṅgerī Śāradā Pīṭha, the address was brought out as a brochure entitled *The Advaitic Notion* by Śrī Śṛṅgerī Śāradā Pīṭha in 1985, and subsequently published under the title *The Advaitic Vision* by Bharatiya Vidya Bhavan, Mumbai.

Having worked under the supervision of Professor Murty for our doctoral researches on Buddhism and Vedānta respectively, and being his younger colleagues in the Department of Philosophy and Religious Studies, we deem it our great privilege to associate with this second edition. While Professor V.V.S. Saibaba is responsible for the transliteration of the Sanskrit verses, Professor P. George Victor has taken care of the editorial aspect of the text. In this context, we are thankful to Professor K. Ramesh of the Department of IRPM in Andhra University, the youngest son of Professor K. Satchidananda Murty for providing the copies of the first editions of these monographs. We are grateful to Shri Susheel K. Mittal, Director of the D.K. Printworld for undertaking the publication under *Andhra University Philosophical Studies* series.

August 9, 2006
Andhra University

V.V.S. Saibaba
P. George Victor

Contents

Part III

The Advaitic Vision

Key to Transliteration

VOWELS

अ *a*	आ *ā*	इ *i*	ई *ī*	उ *u*	ऊ *ū*
(but)	(palm)	(it)	(beet)	(put)	(pool)
ऋ *ṛ*	ए *e*	ऐ *ai*	ओ *o*	औ *au*	
(rhythm)	(play)	(air)	(toe)	(loud)	

CONSONANTS

Guttural	क *ka*	ख* *kha*	ग *ga*	घ *gha*	ङ *ṅa*
	(skate)	(blockhead)	(gate)	(ghost)	(sing)
Palatal	च *ca*	छ* *cha*	ज *ja*	झ *jha*	ञ *ña*
	(chunk)	(catch him)	(john)	(hedgehog)	(bunch)
Cerebral	ट *ṭa*	ठ* *ṭha*	ड *ḍa*	ढ* *ḍha*	ण* *ṇa*
	(start)	(anthill)	(dart)	(godhead)	(under)
Dental	त *ta*	थ *tha*	द *da*	ध* *dha*	न *na*
	(path)	(thunder)	(that)	(breathe)	(numb)
Labial	प *pa*	फ* *pha*	ब *ba*	भ *bha*	म *ma*
	(spin)	(philosophy)	(bin)	(abhor)	(much)
Semi-	य *ya*	र *ra*	ल *la*	व *va*	
vowels	(young)	(drama)	(luck)	(vile)	
Sibilants	श *śa*	ष *ṣa*	स *sa*	ह *ha*	
	(shove)	(bushel)	(so)	(hum)	
Others	क्ष *kṣa*	त्र *tra*	ज्ञ *jña*	ळ* ḷ	ॠ* *ṝ*
	(*kṣatriya*)	(*triśūla*)	(*jñānī*)	(*play*)	

अं (—)*ṁ anusvāra* (nasalisation of preceding vowel) like *saṁskṛti*

अः *visarga* = *ḥ* (aspiration of preceding vowel) like (*prātaḥ*)

ऽ *Avagraha* consonant #'consonant (like:- *ime 'vasthitā*)

Anusvāra at the end of a line is presented by m (म्) and not ṁ

HINDI LETTERS (extras)

ँ = *ñ*	ं = ṅ	ड़ = *ṛa*	ढ़ = *ṛha*
(*candrabindu*)	(*anusvāra*)		

* No exact English equivalents for these letters.

Part I
Hinduism

A man may not believe in God and still call himself a Hindu. Hinduism is a relentless pursuit after truth.

— Mahatma Gandhi

1

The Vision

WE are just now emerging from the throes of a world war. Though technically the war is at an end, if we take note of the situations in Indo-China border, China, Indonesia, Persia and Palestine, as well as in the provinces of our own homeland such as Noakhali, Bombay, Bihar and even Mannargudi and Nalgonda, we cannot with conviction say that the war has stopped. We are, everybody says, on the threshold of a new era. But we have indeed a gloomy prologue of the new era. The world today is passing through the times of unprecedented travail. The ugly racial and communal strife, famine, loot, rapine and murder are found stalking throughout the world. The world is on fire; and when we glance at this phase through which we are passing, we cannot but wonder where we are heading. Deeds of primitive barbarity are being perpetrated in the name of justice and religion. Statesmen and politicians are eagerly devising ways and means to end this miserable state of affairs. Much is being talked about reconstruction and rehabilitation; but what we are actually suffering from is not lack of intelligence, but lack of intuition.

The diabolical subtleties of the atomic and bacteriological warfare of the present age — which the U.S.A. and the Soviet Russia are so proud of — have proved in a striking manner the gigantic intellectual achievements of this generation of Homosapiens. But the wiping out of two cities and the brutal destruction of above two lakh of people at the recent tests carried out at the Bikini Atolls exhibit lamentable lack of feeling and ethical scruples, in short — the degradation of humanity. Universal values have been destroyed. Racial, national and communal ideals have been substituted by short-sighted selfish impulses under the name of patriotism and religion. The trouble is that we are growing greedier and more selfish with the march of time. We are suffering from spiritual blindness. We are having only a one-sided and stunted growth. There is a lacking in vitality and a flagging in spirituality. We have discarded reality and embraced appearance. We have ignored the yolk and clung to the shells. The point is that vain attempts are being made to build the new world-culture and civilization on a one-sided and fundamentally insufficient base. Colossal edifices cannot be constructed on unsound foundations; and no amount of science and art can be maintained without the requisite foundation of humanities. Instead of trying to promote a sense of universal love, which alone can unify humanity as a whole and build-up a better world, captains of the ships of state are still basing their hopes on economic policies and political diplomacies. International co-operation and peace cannot be produced in an American factory, nor can the brotherhood of races be promoted by a five-year plan. As the Apostolic delegate to the East Indies, H.E. Leo Peter Kierkes pointed out in his speech on January 12, 1947 at Bangalore:

> "In this momentous phase of history, ethical and religious values should be held higher than ever, to animate material and economic progress with the spiritual refinement without which civilization and culture have no permanent and ultimate meaning."

Without a spontaneous inner realization, we cannot hope to have real and secure relations with others. We have to realize that the life of our fellowmen is our own life. Close spiritual affinity and a wide tolerant outlook are the only secure basis for human unity. We are all in the grips of materialistic frenzy. Money is amassed with an unparalleled frantic fanaticism. More powerful machines and destructive weapons are being manufactured with a spirit of rivalry unknown in history. Mass production of goods is proceeding in a rapid way. Still the people are frustrated and discontented. They are growing more nervous and bewildered. The simple thing that ought to be kept in mind is that the world is in a state of perpetual exploitation without the unity of humanity. Universal understanding cannot be brought about by force of arms or economic alliances of kingdoms. The Acropolis at Athens, the League of Nations buildings at Geneva and probably the schemes of the United Nations Organization are instances in point. But where economic, political and armed forces fail, there spiritual forces succeed. Where physics ends, metaphysics begins. Invincible is the law of spirit. Victory follows the way of righteousness: *yato dharmaḥ tato jayaḥ*. It is only before the altar of the righteousness that the different people of the globe can swear universal brotherhood. For achieving the righteousness, spiritual reconstruction of the world is more vitally necessary than its material reconstruction. I am gratified when I recollect that no less a personage than the Head of the British Empire, H.M. the King Emperor, realized and emphasized this in his Christmas Day Broadcast when he said:

> "Our task today is to mobilize the spirit and apply its power and healing to our daily life. Devastation and suffering everywhere must move the hearts of all of us, but reconstruction so urgently needed is quite as much spiritual

> as material. It is necessary not merely to rebuild ruined cities and feed hungry people, but also restore the very soul of civilization."

For this tremendous task of mobilizing the spirit and applying its power, a correct understanding of religion and the "study of spirit" are highly necessary. It is because we have ceased to be true Hindus, Muslims or Christians that all these troubles have arisen. We have been misguided by the materialistic life and blinded by it. We are beginning to think that Religion is nothing but a pill of poison. But we should not lose heart. It is one of the inscrutable mysteries of the "Divine" that for short times, the evil triumphs over the good and matter reigns over the spirit. But we should remember that it is a temporary phase; the present is one such. Duryodhana is ruling in all his ill-digested glory and splendour. But we have to remember that Yudhiṣṭhira, the Dharmarāja, is not dead, but in *ajñātavāsa.* The soul of India is not dead. The unbroken spiritual culture and tradition of India, which is distinct and unique and which has been imparting to the world since the last five thousand years, is yet living and shall live. The long line of the carriers of Indian culture from the times of Yājñavalkya and Vaśiṣṭha, through the Buddha and Śaṅkara down to Gandhi and Aurobindo, is continuous and sustained.

Even now, if we awake from the narcotic slumber into which the West has lulled us, and realize the immense potentialities of our religion and culture, we may restore India to her pristine glory. The great poet Iqbal has sung thus:

> *yunān, miśr, rom, sab miṭ gaye jehān se;*
> *bākī magar hai ab tak nāmo niśān hamārā*
> (Where Greece, Egypt and Rome have disappeared,
> there still survive the name and fame of our country.)

The chief need therefore is to understand and imbibe this deep spiritual culture of ours, which is so unique and withstood the ravages of time, and which has been so truly called the *Sanātana Dharma*, the ancient law, which is eternal and holds good for all. It is said that *dharma* is conformity with the truth of things. H.H. Śrī Śaṅkarācārya of Govardhana Pīṭha said:

> "The real principles of Hinduism are not observed as they ought to be; and hence we find so many clashes among Hindus themselves at the present day."

When we do understand our respective religions, we will tend to look upon different religions as mutually complementary. But today, to use the biting words of Swift:

> "We have enough religion to hate one another, but not enough to love one another."

We should put an end to this state of affairs. The mystics say that all of us have a third "eye of wisdom," the *jñāna cakṣu* in addition to the two physical eyes. We should endeavour to see through that spiritual "eye of wisdom"; for when we close it and view the world through these mundane eyes alone, we have but a limited and erroneous vision. Hence it is imperative that everyone should cultivate that integral vision of wisdom, the *jñāna dṛṣṭi*, which alone can bestow upon us toleration, equanimity, poise and catholicity. I beseech you all to cultivate that vision, for as the *Bible* says: "Where there is no vision the people perish."

In order that this moral reconstruction of the World and mobilization of spiritual forces might contribute to the healing of the bruised and bewildered mankind; an all-round education is necessary for all our young men and women. It is one of the evils of the Western civilization that only the intellectual side of education is kept in view. But we have to understand that man is neither brain nor body alone. The individual, we have to understand, is a constituent of body, brain and spirit. If we keep this fact in view, we cannot neglect either the body or spirit. The head and the heart have to keep pace together. A mere one-sided development of the head to the utter neglect of the heart is detrimental. The ideal of education should not only be the enlightenment of the intellect, but also the inspiration of the heart. If half the amount of budget and money that is being spent on national laboratories and industrial workshops is spent on the cultivation of the spirit, the world would in no time be a thousand-fold happier. What is required is a proper integration of the two sides of education — the spiritual and the material, the humanities and sciences. Only then our spirits can walk with our intellects.

Here comes the need for religious education; and in India, the need is especially greater than anywhere, because ours is a country inhabited by people of different religious faiths; and to a great extent it is the religion that determines the political, economic and social relations of our countrymen. True religion is meant to and ought to cement mankind together. In these circumstances all educated men should understand the nature and the basic principles of religion. In this context, it will be impossible to improve upon what former chief minister Mr Tanguturi Prakasam said in his convocation address to the students of Andhra University:

> "It is therefore necessary, in the circumstances in which we are placed today, that all those educated by Universities and colleges should get a real insight into the different religions and understand the essential oneness of them, become tolerant of each other and teach tolerance to the masses to whom they stand in the position of guides and mentors. Nor is the study of religion incompatible or inconsistent with the study of science. . . . If we understand

> and study religion properly, we will be doing a great service to ourselves and to the people at large. This is the need of the hour. Statesmen may think of other remedies to combat communalism. But their remedies are bound to be superficial and mechanical."

Mr Prakasam continued:

> "I feel that a student should be taught the essence of all religions from the formative age right up to the University stage to bring about a happy state of affairs."

A reorientation of the fundamental problems of life and a moral reconstruction of the world towards a spiritual fraternity of nations is the crying need of the hour. Only then can the tangles of the present-day world be solved. To this end, the "study of the spirit" should form the compulsory part of college curriculum. For, as Yogi Vemana has said:

> *cadivi cadivi cadivi cāvaṅga netiki?*
> *cavu leni caduvu caduva valayu.*
>
> Why study, study, study until death?
> Study the studies of deathlessness

We should follow the instruction that give immortal life to man. This can be achieved by paying an equally sincere devotion to the much neglected but most needed religious instruction. Religion is not a belief in a set of anti-scientific and irrational dogmas. Religion in its theoretical aspect is the study of spirit, while in its practical aspect it is righteous living. To inculcate the principles of right living and to prepare our young men and women for their vast future responsibilities, our universities and colleges should impart religious education compulsorily. I am happy when I remember that so eminent an educationist as Dr Lakshmanaswami Mudaliar, Vice

Chancellor of the Madras University, has expressed the same opinion in his presidential address to the All India Educational Conference at Trivandrum. He says:

> "I am a great believer in the value of religious education and hold to the firm conviction that a life divorced from a religious background lacks the sheet-anchor which will enable man to steady himself against the billows and hollows of world's surging tides."

The aim of this religious education should not be the promotion of isolationism or sectarianism. Our religion should not teach us to hate another's religion, nor should our adherence to a particular sub-sect of a religion make us to hate another's sub-sect. The understanding of our religion should be so deep and real that we should be able to recognize and respect other's religion. As Mr Liaqat A.H. Khan has observed in his book on *Muslim Educational Problems*:

> "A good Hindu and a good Muslim or Christian who have been properly brought up in the traditions of their faiths are always good neighbours and live on terms of amity and mutual regard."

In short, the ideal is the cultivation of the spiritual vision. The vision is essentially a global outlook as contrasted with the mental outlook which is one-sided because it is the view from one or a few angles alone. Ordinarily, however highly informed or educated he may be, man has a fixed standpoint, an *idee fixe.* He is blind to the simple truth that in relation to a problem there are various standpoints; that any one of them can be adopted with equal impunity; and that others might adopt a different standpoint from his. Spiritual consciousness begins where this limited mental outlook ends. Cultivation of the vision, in other words, is the coming out of one's own shell of egoism. The intellect and its external drive (*parañci kāni vyatrunāt svayaṁ bhuḥ*) make us to perceive only a single line of thought and action, often superficial. Even that which appears sometimes as evil and reprehensible to our circumscribed outlook may have goodness and beauty in its core. To come out of one's ulterior consciousness and to enter into the universal and inner consciousness and see things as others see them is the dawn of a "divine life." As Manu has beautifully expressed it: "This is mine, this is his — this sort of compartmentalization is the nature of the ill-informed. For the enlightened (*udara)* the whole world is one family": *udara caritanam tu vasudhaiva kuṭumbakam.*

The vision is not global in the sense that it is the sum-total or aggregate of all imperfect and superficial views. It is global in the sense that it manifests the one dynamic truth which underlies everything and which manifests itself in diverse ways, expressing itself in multiple means. When we achieve this vision, the integral view, then disparities and divisions disappear, and contraries and incompatibles become complementary and corollary to each other. When one has realized this supreme truth, one enters into the Universal consciousness. His divine-eye, *divya-cakṣu,* is opened and inevitably and naturally finds "himself in all beings and all beings in himself," *sarva bhūteṣu ca ātmānām, sarvabhūtāni ca ātmani.* The brotherhood of man then but becomes an appendix to this supreme discovery — the truth of the identity (*tādātmya*) of the individual soul (*jīvātmā*) with the universal soul (*viśvātmā*). Only then our ancient Aryan ideal of *ṣamatā sarvatra,* "equanimity everywhere" can materialize. Then only the kingdom of Heaven can be ushered in.

2

The Rise of Religion

THERE is a very old saying, that we never know a thing unless we know its beginning. We may know a great deal about Islam or Hinduism, we may read all the sacred texts, the creeds and catechisms. All said and done is true; but we will be unable to grasp the principles and nature of religion unless we know the original springs wherefrom it flows. A book on geology or astronomy generally begins with the definitions for the questions of, "what is geology"? and "what is astronomy?" We cannot write on minerals or planets without first explaining what a mineral or a planet is. It is the same with religion. Without knowing what religion meant, we cannot discuss it.

The word *religion* is derived from *re-legere*, which indicates "to gather up again," "to take up," "to consider," "to ponder." Thus religion originally meant gathering up and considering carefully. To ponder, to reflect or meditate was therefore the original meaning of religion, as opposed to *Intelligo* which meant connecting together, arranging or classifying.

According to Kant, religion is morality, while religion is knowledge for Fichte. On the other hand Schleiermacher defined religion as dependence on something, which though it determines us cannot in turn be determined by us. Hegel asserted that religion is or ought to be perfect freedom. Later Comte declared that man cannot know anything higher than man; and therefore for man, as a class, humanity is the true object of religious knowledge and worship. Feurbach has gone further and substituted the individual man for collective man. Self-love according to him is the universal principle and law, which religion confirms on every page of its history.

We see thus that no two thinkers agree in defining religion. The trouble is that each has seen only one aspect of it to the neglect of the others. We cannot deny, of course, when Kant says that religion is morality, nor when Fichte says religion is knowledge. But none can oppose Feurbach when he says that religion is self-love. Religion is all this and yet more.

Religion first arose when man came face to face with the limitless, the Infinite. The beginning of religion can be traced to the surprised and innocent looks of the Poiynesian sailors when they first cast their glances on the endless expanses of the ocean. It can be traced to the jubilant outbursts of the Aryan shepherds when they greeted the resplendent effulgence of the dawn in the spotless blue skies of the land of Sapta-Sindhu. It began when in the bare and boundless sandy deserts of Egypt and Arabia, the last rays from the sinking surface of the setting sun fell upon the fascinated eyes of the fatigued and solitary traveller. It was the reactions of these innocent souls, which formed the first chapter in the history of religion.

There have been anthropological and sociological accounts of the beginning of religion. For, what the anthropologists and ethnologists are searching for in the practices of the South American or central Australian primitives constitutes the beginning of ritualistic religion. But what we have to understand is that religion is not ritual. When the naked savages of the south-eastern Australia dance, shouting, *daramulan, daramulan* or when the pious old Hindus offer cooked rice balls to their departed ancestors, is it religion? Religion is neither ritual, nor custom. When we transcend ritual, we do have religion. The anthropologists are seriously and grievously erring when they confound ritual with religion and give us what is known as the evolution of religion, when in fact they are but describing the genesis and growth of custom or ritual. We have to bear in mind that theology transcends anthropology.

Religion is neither a faith nor a belief or a set of dogmas. It is this wrong understanding of religion that has led to the crusades and religious persecutions in Europe. Judaism with its belief in a "jealous god" and a "chosen people" has sown the poisonous germ first, which later infected Christianity and Islam, and on their turn responsible for all the conflicts between different religions. The Hindu conception of religion is fortunately very different. If by religion is meant the adherence of people to a particular form of ritual, belief or faith with a set of theological dogmas, then there is no such thing as Hindu religion; because those who practice different and antagonistic forms of rituals, such as the Śāktas, the Śaivas and the Vaiṣṇavas are Hindus. In spite of this, Hindus consist of pluralists and monists, monistic-pluralists, and so on. In fact, a Hindu need not believe at all in the existence of a godhead, either personal or impersonal. That is why among the six orthodox systems of Hindu thought, three are atheistic undoubtedly. If Absolutism is also atheism, then the thinker who speaks of the god-head as a phenomenal necessity and relative reality (*vyavahārika satyam*) — Śaṅkara and the Advaita Vedānta are also atheistic.

People who worship different gods or the same god in different ways and people who worship no god at all are all Hindus. In the words of Radhakrishnan "the theist, the atheist, the sceptic and the agnostic may all be Hindus if they accept the Hindu system of culture and life." There are only polytheistic or theistic religions. Hinduism is the only exception to this. It embraces both these but rises above them. Hinduism, we can say, is Supra-Theistic.

As the *Kūrma Purāṇa* says, here we have people who worship different gods and adopt different rituals: *nānā devārcane yukta, nānā karmāṇi kūrvate*. But now we have to initiate research as to how so many different communities, who practised different rites, worshipped different gods and who were spread over the continent became woven into a single cultural pattern with a common history and spirit. At times the whole of primitive tribes were absorbed into the Hindu-fold. They brought in their own ideas and worshipped their own gods. In spite of all this, Hindus have a common culture, a definite view of life and an integral unity. "That unity transcends the innumerable diversities of blood, colour, language, dress, manners and sect," observes Vincent Smith in his *History of India*. All this has been possible because of the Hindu conception of religion.

Religion is *dharma* or conformity to the law according to Hindus. The perception of "Reality" face to face (*darśana*) and the experience of it is also religion. Only he who actually does this is truly religious. But this experience should neither be subjective nor emotional. The convictions which are the results of our experience, should appeal to our intellect. Our reason should give credit to our experience, or else our experience becomes hallucination. Only in such an experience, we should have faith. Spiritual perception is no exception to the laws of logic. Spiritual experiences, when interpreted rationally, should not go contrary to the nature and laws of our everyday life. We need not believe anything simply if a sacred book says so or a holy man ordains. Wesley has said:

> "What is faith? not an opinion or any number of opinions put together, be they ever so true. It is the vision of the soul, that power by which spiritual things are apprehended just as material things are apprehended by the physical senses."

Hinduism does not value the attitude that is said to have been adopted by the Grand Caliph, when he destroyed the great library at Alexandria. It does not say that the Veda is to be respected because it is revealed. The Vedas are sacred and are to be held in high esteem, because they are records of the experiences of the seers, which can be re-experienced on any day, by sincere compliance with certain conditions. As Vācaspati observes in his *Bhāmatī* that the Vedas are to be valued not just because they are traditional, but when they have the strength of perception and support of logic: *tātparyavati śruti, pratyakṣād balavatī, na śruti mātram*. The Vedas are the records of the spirit of our forefathers along with some of their beliefs and views; and some of which appear ridiculous today. But this is inevitable. Nowhere can we procure the grain without the husk, the egg without its shell and the rose without its thorns. Just because the Vedas are ancient with the cobwebs that have grown around them, we need not necessarily reject everything in the Vedas. In other words, as Kālidāsa said, neither all that which is ancient need be treated as perfect just because it is ancient, nor everything novel need be deemed imperfect just because it is novel: *purāṇam iti eva na sādhu sarvam, na ca api sarvam navam iti avādyam*. Einstein's physics need not be less true or accurate just because it is modern, nor Newton's physics is perfect and infallible just because it is old. If other branches of knowledge like science grow, surely theology can develop. Physics may have mathematics as its base, but the study of religion can never have mathematics as its basis. As such we cannot say that only that which is said in the *Qurān* or the Vedas is the last word. Our ancients realized this when they said, *anantaḥ vai vedaḥ*, "endless is the Veda." It is valid not because it was revealed in the dim ages of the past, but because it can be experienced even now. It is everlastingly eternal, because it voices the eternal truth: *vācā virūpa nityayā*. Nor is it authoritative because it derives its sanctity from God or any other external source. It is authoritative because it can be practised and felt, here and now; it is *svataḥ-siddha*. The centre of gravity in Hinduism is on experience, and not on authority. Hinduism begins and ends in *anubhava*, experience.

Veda is that which makes itself known: *vedayati iti vedaḥ*. It is self-luminous knowledge. It is hidden in our own consciousness: *guhāyām nihitaḥ*. When the individual's exterior intellectual drive turns inward, when one is free from the shackles of the limitations of form and process then the bud of knowledge hidden deeply in the cavity of heart will bloom through successive stages of experience. But unless there is that seed of *a priori* knowledge in one's own mind, no amount of external stimulation can make it grow into full knowledge. No amount of hatching can produce the chicken, without the egg being there.

Generally it is the word (*śabda Brahman*) that uncovers the sheaths of the bud of knowledge and makes it bloom. It might be the inner or outer word. In either case its role is merely to impart the necessary momentum to the *gupta jñāna*, hidden knowledge. For the majority of people, an outer word is necessary. They cannot inspire themselves by themselves. Only a Siddhārdha could sit alone, grapple with the problem and arrive at a solution. Others need the Buddha to inspire them. Without an inspiring outer word, many cannot realize themselves. The external stimulations for our consciousness can either come from an ancient book or from a living preceptor.

It was the *Bible* which awakened Thomas, and it was the Upaniṣads which roused Schopenhauer. But it was Ramakrishna who illumined Vivekānanda and Nārada who inspired Vālmikī.

Many are not lucky enough to find a preceptor of the calibre of a Nārada or a Ramakrishna. For them the resort is the oral or written word, the Śruti or the *Bible* which has helped many, which has gained sanctity on account of its potentiality to transmit its message through successive generations of men. That is why the *Bhagavad-Gītā* says that the scripture shall be the refuge in case of doubt or perplexity: *tasmāt śāstram pramāṇam te.* To comprehend "Reality" in its multiple ways, in its successive stages and graded forms, we have to resort to the *śabda*, word. Since the majority of us cannot listen to our inner voice, we need the traditional word, Veda or Śruti, which has shown its worth by lifting many a generation of our forefathers. The Śrutis, as Radhakrishnan has put it, are the precious echoes of God's voice in the souls of men of long ago. Accordingly it rests upon us to see that we properly interpret and understand the Veda, so that what it says is not in conflict with the findings of science or the dictates of our unprejudiced reason. Where tradition goes contrary to the actual state of things, it should be modified and if need be supplanted. Where assumptions go contrary to experiments, they should be damned. The rules applicable to science, be it empirical or spiritual, are the same. Religion is neither ritual nor belief in dogma, but an experience and enjoyment. Further, to ignite and dynamite our personality and make it experience and enjoy the religious truth, to ignite our lethargic consciousness, to expand the coiled serpent-like spiral of power hidden in all of us (the *kuṇḍalinī*), a teacher (*guru*) or a traditional word (*mantra*) is necessary. The Veda fulfils this necessity.

But one thing we have overlooked. If religion is experience, then the question arises: experience of what? The experience of the Boundless, the Unlimited, the Absolute, the Divine — the *mahān* or the *bṛhat*.

I might be excused if I become a little autobiographical, to explain the matter. When I was in Pondicherry a year and a half ago, I was staying in a hotel overlooking the sea. On the first night of my sojourn, I was unable to get sleep due to the newness of the place. When however I got it somehow, I was disturbed at midnight. Unable to sleep, I got up and gazed through the window. It was the last day of the black-fortnight. There was no moon, the stars were shining bright. The limitless expanse of the whitish blue and sombre ocean stretched away from me for miles and miles. It was the first time, I gazed at the ocean at midnight and at such close quarters. I was overwhelmed by the vast and boundless canopy of the blackish blue sky littered with countless stars above and by the endless black sheet of water roaring rhythmically with white foamy waves below. I was neither frightened nor was I awed or amazed. I simply felt lost. I lost my individuality. I felt I was no longer existent. The infiniteness of the sky and the sea and the monotonous rhythm of the roar simply swallowed me up. In the *Bible*, it is recorded: "my zeal for the Lord has eaten me up." Intellect ceased to function and intuition became active. I was doing nothing, saying nothing and thinking nothing. In short I was experiencing nothing, nothing whatsoever particular. Does that not mean that I was experiencing everything, everything universal? That is the beginning of religious experience and it is not subjective because it can be repeated by anyone.

The religious experience, as has been earlier pointed out, began when in the days of yore the Aryan youths tending their cows and sheep in the fertile plains of Indus and its tributaries first saw the dawn. They saw the shining sun rise in all its splendour, casting its rosette rays on the snow-clad Himalayas, painting them purple and gold and violet. Their hearts melted as did the snow of Himalayas. Their minds grasped what they could not express. They were lost in infinity. They became one with infinity. But this lasted only for a few moments. When they recovered and came back to themselves with perspiring skins and raised hairs, they fell down on their knees and said:

> *tat savitur vareṇyam bhargo devasya dhīmahi* ।
>
> we contemplate, O sun, on thy majestic and covetable grandeur.
>
> *dhiyo yo naḥ pracodayāt* ।
>
> Quicken thou our intellects.

The first *samādhi* occurred thus and the song of the soul, or to use Max Müller's words "the oldest prayer of the world," was uttered then. It is this same prayer, which in other words was later voiced again and again in the Upaniṣads. In multifarious vestures and in sophisticated garbs it appeared again as the psalms in Judea and as the *stotra*s in India.

This phenomenon might be in different forms, repeated itself in the valleys of Nile and the plains of Amazon. In intensity and variety it might have differed, but almost in a similar strain arose religious experience in every land. The "Infinite" first revealed itself to different races in different ways. But the process and content of revelation everywhere is identical. To the pastoral Vedic poets, it revealed itself in the phenomena of nature, in Dawn, in sunset and in the thunderstorm. To some races the "Infinite" intimated itself in the birth of a child or the death of the beloved. To some it revealed itself in the abyss of their own hearts. Beautiful are Sri Aurobindo's stanzas that can be quoted in this context:

> In the blue of the sky, in the green of the forest
> Whose is the hand that painted the glow?
> When the winds were asleep in the womb of the ether,
> Who was it roused them and bade them flow?"
>
> He is lost in the heart, in the cavern of Nature,
> He is found in the brain where he builds up thought;
> In the pattern and bloom of the flowers He is woven,
> In the luminous net of the stars He is caught.

Or again as Wordsworth has said and said so well,

> Obstinate questionings,
> of sense and outward things,
> Fallings from us, vanishings,
> Blank misgivings of a creature
> Moving about in worlds not realized.

Thus arose the first experience of the Divine, the "Infinite." But when the seers came out of their visions and were questioned as to what they saw or felt, they were unable to explain. When pressed to define the nature of what he saw, the *ṛṣi* of the Upaniṣads replied, *santo yam ātma* "The Absolute is silence." When Yājñavalkya was similarly questioned, he said, "The eye goes not there, neither does speech reach it; the mind ceases to function there; and we know not how to teach it to others."

The inability on the part of the seers and mystics to describe in words what they have experienced roused suspicions in sceptic minds. Surely if one has experienced something one must be able to tell it. But not so always is the case. Can we translate into words the ecstatic rapture of the sexual embrace?

And simply because it cannot be expressed through speech, are we justified in saying that the happiness of the sexual embrace is subjective? Or can the impotent man or sterile woman deny the existence at all of sexual happiness, since he or she has not experienced it? Similar is the case with mystic experience, which embraces the Divine and enjoys it in intimate contact. It is neither subjective, just because it is inexpressible in words, nor is it unreal just because we have not so far felt its glow and radiant warmth. The great mystic Ruysbroeck described the Divine as "the dim silence where all lovers lose themselves."

But in this self-contented silence, *niḥśabdatā*, man cannot afford to remain forever. Though the seer is aware that "silence is more significant than speech regarding the depths of the Divine," he cannot but speak of it. Man's chief prerogative over his nearest animals, the anthropod apes, is the power of articulating speech. He feels a particular exultation in the exercise of his tongue. So he endeavours to describe his religious experience too. But how to do it? How to intelligize the intuited? How to define the Indefinite? Intellect craves to understand; and to understand means to define, to delimit. So the Divine is spoken of in terms of the most non-qualitative qualities. The pure being *sat*, is associated with *cit* and *ānanda.* So the supreme is understood as being, bliss and beatitude, *sat-cid-ānanda*. Even this conception is too sublime, as sublime as the Pyramid. Man cannot constantly be gazing at the real Pyramid. To imagine the supreme as a vast ocean of *cit* and *ānanda* is a strain for the intellect. So imagination aids intellect, and the Infinite, the Boundless, has become God, the limited. As the Upaniṣads put it, "Thus is God created and fashioned by the heart, the understanding and the mind." The highest category that can be conceived is personality; and we are all persons. Therefore God is necessarily the perfect personality, *puruṣottama.* What we have got, he has got in abundance. We have some knowledge and some power. So he is omniscient and omnipotent. This anthropomorphization does not stop there. Colours are conjoined and the ideal is materialized; and the picture of a still more personal God is drawn on the canvas of mind. God is at this stage imagined as a supremely beautiful super-human being, with all auspicious qualities (*ananta-kalyāṇa guṇa*) inherent in Him. He becomes Viṣṇu or Kṛṣṇa. Name and form are attributed to Him, who is nameless and formless. Functions, such as the creation of the world, and the destruction of it are invested in Him. The Absolute, the *Brahman*, becomes Viṣṇu Puruṣottama, with all auspicious qualities.

But the movement of the materialization of the ideal, the humanization of the "Divine," the anthropomorphization of the "Theos," does not stop there. Sometimes the human mind does not stop till it has vulgarized the sublime and has degraded it beyond redemption. What can we say when the student fails to get pass marks, fasts, and says it is *satyāgraha*? Can we imagine a greater profanation of the Gandhian concept of *satyāgraha*? But such is the tendency of the human mind. Minor gods, if not gods, angels, archangels, demons, kings of demons and universes to sustain all these imaginary hordes; priests to procure us interviews with these imaginary gods; and ways to propitiate these gods, and means to avoid the anger of the anti-gods, are all imagined with such an intensity, that we almost come to believe these hallucinations of ours to be true. This is what has happened. This is religion as popularly understood, religion at its worst, nay irreligion. There is as much difference between this adulterated form of religion and true religion as between Ganges water flowing on the summits of Himalaya near Kedāra and Gaṅgotrī and Gaṅges water with all its accumulated dirt flowing near Calcutta and its suburbs.

I know that an anthropological or a sociological account of the genesis and growth of religion has not been furnished; never was it my intention. I defined religion as the "science of spirit." It has then its prologue in the sudden ecstatic awareness of the "Infinite" and the "Boundless." It has therefore its epilogue in the repeated and sustained rapturous experience of the "Divine."

3

The Vedānta

THE philosophic principles of Hinduism are chiefly contained in the Vedānta texts: the Upaniṣads, the *Brahma-Sūtras* and the *Bhagavad-Gītā*. These three together form the supreme authority for the Hindu religion, and are known as the *prasthāna-trayī* of the Vedānta. As the popular verse has it, "minor scriptures sink into silence when the Vedānta roars, as do the foxes when the lion roars":

> *tāvad garjanti śāstrāṇi jambūka vipene yathā* ।
> *nagarjāti mahāśaktiḥ yāvad vedānta kesarī* ॥

All the teachings of the Upaniṣads converge in the realization of the "Infinite." But no metaphysic is valid till it is supported by logic. The *Brahma-Sūtras* endeavours to do this job. Our realization of the "Divine" should be such as to make our lives more divine and therefore more worth living. The consummation of the integral vision is complete only when our realization of the "Divine" works itself out in the politico-social everyday affairs of ours. The *Bhagavad-Gītā* shows how spiritual philosophy can be practically applied. It teaches how the supreme purpose can be realized in the affairs of men. On the philosophical bases of the Upaniṣads, the *Bhagavad-Gītā* erects its theory of spiritual dynamism. Only when spirituality expresses in disinterested activism, it is really ripe and perfect. As Benedetto Croce has so beautifully said:

> Religion and Philosophy, the practical and the theoretical, life and thought, form the eternal rhythm of the spirit.

The doctrine of the Upaniṣads is essentially an intuitional one. According to them, truth has many faces: *satyam viśvatomukham.* It is a scintillating gem, a Kohinoor, scattering its million shining rays in all directions. Dazzled by but one of its million rays, man thinks that he has seen the diamond in its entirety, while what he has seen is but the glare of one of its innumerable rays. He, satisfied that he has obtained a photo of the gem in his own mind, falls into a colossal blunder, while to speak the fact he has but secured only a caricature of it. Intellect, we have to realize, is inherently incapable and insufficient to grasp the whole. Whenever ultimate questions arise intellect confesses itself to be inadequate. Intellect functions through the categories of space and time, cause and force, which are but myths and conventions, symbols and shibboleths. It is all right as long as we are analysing and trying to understand the empirical experience. But when intellect tries to cast off the shackles that it has itself erected, when it tries to pierce to the core through the conceptions of space and time, it shows its poverty and bankruptcy; and again as psychologists and anthropologists fully well known, that we think almost in words. Actual and real knowledge cannot be had through ideas and much less from words. Only when we burrow to the roots of our ideas, we can get at real knowledge. Thought gives us only imperfect and distorted pictures of reality. Intellectual perception is inevitably one-sided. That is why we have different philosophies. The conflicts of these diverse systems of philosophy are existing because all of them depend upon mind and logic. But logic and reason fail to attain reality. Reality is neither an idea nor a conception. So it is beyond thought. Only when thought is brought to a standstill and intellect ceases to function realizing its limitations, then, beyond the antinomies that confront us, beyond the deadlocks that confound us and beyond the oppositions that confuse us, we can view reality as it is. When intellect is perfected in intuition, we have the vision. If we fail to realize this and engage ourselves in intellectual acrobatics and lingual jugglery, we will be at no solution. One day we have to realize, as did the wise Omar Khayyam said, that intellect is an unsatisfactory instrument to comprehend reality:

> When young did eagerly frequent
> Doctor and saint, and heard great argument
> About it and about, yet ever more —
> Came out by the same door wherein I went.

This is so because thought is relative. But reality is absolutely one, and not related to anything else, because it is itself the synthesis or the unified organic totality of everything. As such intellect which is essentially relative cannot grasp the relationless whole. As the Upaniṣads said, "neither speech nor even the mind can reach it." So the Upaniṣads posit that we cannot grasp this central "spiritual reality" in this empirical and mundane way. The spirit can be discerned only spiritually. Only when we scale the systems of thought rising one over another like Alps over Alps, our sightseeing culminates in the view of "absolute reality." The distinctions of intellect and the riddles of reason have to be surpassed. When we transcend reasoning and reach religion, we get it. As the Upaniṣads say, neither genius nor much learning can aid us in getting at the core of reality: *na medhayā, na bahunā śrutena.* No amount of useless activity or fruitless discussion can reap the harvest of the spirit. When the mind stops functioning and its thought ceases then real knowledge of spirit dawns. When the shades of night fall thick, Minerva's owl sees solemn. When all the traffic in the streets is arrested, the king comes in a procession. So also when the heavy mental traffic, that is, our thoughts, wishes, willing, desires etc., is arrested then truth in its unparalleled richness and splendour flashes. Yoga is the practical discipline to put an end to the wavering of the mind: *yogaḥ citta vr̥tti nirodhaḥ*. To comprehend the supra-mental reality, we have to cross the limitations of mind. So long as we depend on our mental faculties, we get but distorted and incorrect visions of reality. When once mental faculties are curbed and kept under control, truth dawns thereon. We get then the integral vision, whereupon we will neither be dismayed by divergences nor swayed by difficulties. It is this experience and the highest knowledge that is recorded in the Upaniṣads. As has been already pointed out earlier, unlike perceptual knowledge and experience this is impossible to be formulated in words. To the man that is born blind, we cannot explain the beauties of a rainbow. One has but to see it and feel it. It is for this reason that the Upaniṣads throughout exhort us to resort to Yoga. But it should be understood that nowhere do the Upaniṣads scorn the intellect. The intellect is neither a useless nor a misguiding faculty. It is of the highest value so long as its limitations are known. One thing that has to be remembered is that intellect is not the all-powerful panacea. Reason's realm has to be recognized, but its domain has to be demarcated. It has also a thus-far and no-farther. No doubt it can visage reality and its account of reality is not false; but only incomplete. Imperfection is not falsity. Intellect, of course, does not investigate the unreal, neither does it scrutinize the absolute real. Intellect is fulfilled in and perfected by intuition. The intuitional and the mystical are not the contradictory of the intellectual and the logical, but the subsumptive of it. The intuitive method of the Upaniṣads is supra-rational, not sub-rational. As the consummation of the bud is in the fruit and the end of virginity lies in motherhood, so too the ideal of the intellect becomes the real in intuition. Intellect devoid of intuition is unfinished and fragmentary, while intuition unaided by intellect is empty and dark. That is why the *Īśa Upaniṣad* enjoins upon us the need for the correlation of *vidyā* with *avidyā*, the attainment of which unifies, embraces and fuses all the paradoxes and contradictions which stare us at day in and day out. Then we shall have no place for Kant's antinomies or Bradley's contradictions. They will simply become mutual complementaries supporting the one fundamental reality.

The same conclusion has been reached by an examination of the present state of scientific knowledge by scientists of the calibre of Jeans, Eddington and even Einstein. Reality transcends the physico-chemical sciences. They analyse only form and process. But they cannot go to the thing-in-itself. As the traveller riding in the desert blinded by the dust raised by himself feels that the whole desert is filled by that dust itself, the physicist too cannot get at the reality not only because of the circumscribed mentality of his but also because of the limitations of his own instruments and assumptions. As Einstein has correctly said, science is but the deduction of one unknown thing from another unknown thing. This is the state of the physio-chemical sciences, which are supposed to be very highly developed. The relativity theory has superseded the gravitation theory, which had been considered perfect for centuries; and who dares to pronounce this to be the final verdict? Already Whitehead and a few others are trying to modify, supplement or reinterpret it; when progress in these sciences itself is like this, nothing need be said of the bio-social sciences; the less we talk of them the better.

Now we can understand how it is that truth has eluded the profoundest thinkers and the greatest scientists, and why it has chosen to bare itself to the seers alone. It is because they have cultivated the necessary conditions for comprehending truth in all its vastness. As Paul Brunton has pointed out: "Thinkers have made admirable attempts, but they have failed to win success because they lacked the tool of a *yoga*-equipped, ego-purified and body-subdued mentality with which to force open the shut-gates of truth." Only when we discard our sophistication, our learning and our reasoning, in short, only when we become like children, we can hope to enter the portals of truth:

tasmād brāhmaṇaḥ pāṇḍityam nirvidyā bālyena tiṣṭhaset ।
— *Bṛhadāraṇyaka Upaniṣad*

Question now arises: What is the conclusion that the *ṛṣis* of the Upaniṣads have arrived at? What is the central teaching of the Upaniṣads? The avenues of approach to the problem of ultimate reality are three.

First: The unsophisticated naïve mind of man, when it sees the forces of nature in all their fury and nakedness imagines them to be the ultimate realities. At this stage, the sun, the moon and the lightning, etc. are considered to be the ultimate realities. But soon deeper reflection and greater insight into events will make us learn that natural phenomena by themselves are not "Reality" as such. Gradually we tend to probe deeper. Soon we inevitably come to the conclusion that behind the cosmos there must be a something, a verity, an existence (*sattā*) which is the origin, the sustainer and the end of everything: *yato vā imāni bhūtāni jāyante, yena jātāni jīvanti, yat prayānti abhisaṁviśanti.* As soon as this idea strikes us, we cannot but believe that there is something, from which the world has sprung — the Absolute. The *Chāndogya Upaniṣad* expresses the entire conception of the Absolute by a single word, *tajjalan*, which indicates that from the Absolute the world has originated, that it is in it that it is sustained and that it is finally in it that it is dissolved. As soon as the existence of an ultimate verity behind the cosmos is recognized, it has to be also recognized as the fountain source of all energy, which is found in the world. The forces of nature, the wind, the fire, the lightning, etc. — which the ignorant deem to be independent appear but as the manifestations of the ultimate power and energy — the Absolute. As the *Kena Upaniṣad* says, it is the power of *Brahman* which flashes in the lightning and it is the same power which manifests itself in the activities of the mind and thinks. In short, the Absolute is to be conceived not only as the ultimate existence behind the cosmos, but also as the primal unmanifested energy, which expresses itself in the phenomena of nature and the working of mind. This is necessary because as soon as we say that the Absolute is the fundamental substratum of the universe and stop there, we tend to think that the Absolute is a dead static entity to avoid which it is to be conceived as the unmanifested Supreme power or Energy (*Parāśakti*). The nature of this energy, the Upaniṣads tell us, is supreme radiance and sublime luminosity. It is pure light (*cit*). It is not simply an abyss, a dark night wherein a black cow and a white cow cannot be distinguished. It is the primal source of all light and radiance to which the sun and the moon, the stars, the lightning and the fire owe their resplendent splendour. The so-called shining objects derive their power of illumination from the Absolute. It is by its luminosity that they are illuminated: *tasya bhāsa sarvam idam vibhāti*. The *Brahman* of the Absolute is to be conceived, if it is to be conceived, as the fundamental of all existence, as the origin of all energy and as the source of all radiance. It is *sat* and also *cit*. It is the subtle essence of all things, of which all of them are but gross manifestations. When we go behind the second causes, when the veils fall apart, we realize that it is the same subtle essence which underlies everything. The famous dialogue of Śvetaketu and his father Uddālaka deserves to be quoted here:

> "Bring me the yonder fruit of *nyagrodha*." "I have brought it, Sir." "Break it." "It is broken, Sir." "What do you see here?" "Seeds, Sir, infinite in number and infinitesimal in size." "Break one of them." "It is broken, Sir." "What do you see now?" "Nothing, Sir." "My dear fellow, it is from that subtle essence which is not perceived by you, that this *nyagrodha* tree is made. Believe it, my boy. It is of that subtle essence that everything is filled. It is the truth. It is the self; and, thou, O Śvetaketu, art that" ("O Śvetaketu, *tat tvaṁ asi*)."

The dialogue drives home the truth of the unity of all life; and hence the oneness of the life of man with that of universe. Because, it is from the same unmanifested subtle essence that the great *nyagrodha* tree and also everything else in the world have evolved. As such the existence of the cosmos is also the essence of man: *piṇḍāṇḍa* = *Brahmāṇḍa*. Since it is the same essence that underlies all the things of the world, the whole world is a universe and not plural-universes; and further both the physical and mental worlds are but manifestations of the same subtle essence, *Brahman*. Thus we arrive at the conception of the Absolute, as pure existence which is the original source of all energy and radiance and also as the subtle but same essence which is at the back of everything; and on what does the Absolute rest? The Upaniṣad replies that it rests on its own greatness: *sa sve mahimni pratiṣṭhitaḥ*. Who can rule the ruler? The Infinite rests on infinity and depends thereon. It encompasses everything and embraces the All. It is neither dependent on anything nor is derived from anything. It was at the beginning: *sat eva saumya idam agre āsīt.* It is pure energy and pure luminosity.

The above is a meagre outline as to how we arrive at the conception of the Absolute cosmologically. The same conception can be arrived at theologically and also psychologically.

Second: Primitive mind tends to personify every phenomenon which strikes or arrests it. The beauty of the sunset or the dawn strikes us. We personify the event, and give it a name. We begin to worship the concept. So too the grandeur of a hill or the beauty of a forest profoundly influences us. We personify them, baptise them and begin to adore the hill or the forest. Thus originate gods. In course of time they become so numerous, that we can hardly count them. This sort of thing is unsatisfactory to intellect. The inevitable culmination of the quest after God is monotheism. The Supreme can only be one. There cannot be a number of presiding deities; and even if many deities are to be admitted, the ultimate Deity can only be one, because there cannot be two beings with unlimited power and knowledge. The pantheon too should have a president. The unrivalled one only can be the God. If the several phenomena of nature demand separate deities, the unity of nature points towards one single God. The belief in an order prevailing in nature and the design which is apparent in nature call for faith in the one God. The quest after the discovery of a single creative principle, which is itself uncreated, terminates in the conception of a single controlling spirit, which alone regulates the workings of the whole universe. Then, all the various gods are merged in the one God Himself. Thus we arrive at the truth that though various are the names, the principle is after all one: *ekam sat vipraḥ* *bahudhā vadanti.* But human mind cannot stop here. We cannot be satisfied with the description of God as a benevolent despot sitting on His golden throne with the gilded sceptre in His hand, in the heaven surrounded by angels. Why should He be in heaven only? Has He also the limitations under which we labour? Is He capable of occupying only a definite space? If so, how is He different from the other persons and things? Is He not the Unlimitable, the Infinite, the *ananta*? Need He be confined to heaven alone? Cannot He be present everywhere at the same time? Does He too labour under the physical disabilities and impossibilities which surround us? The Upaniṣads answer that He, the God, is present in all things, in fire, in earth, in water, nay, in all the universe: *yo agnau yo apsu, yo viśvambhuvanam aviveṣa.* The *Chāndogya Upaniṣad* says that He pervades the whole world and is immanent in it just as salt pervades the waters of the ocean through and through. The supreme reality moves in all things living in all. Now if God is immanent in everything, if it is indeed He who shines in the sun, blushes in the rose, thunders in the storm and rides in the gales, is it not He that verily animates the human body too? The Upaniṣads assert in the affirmative. Only when He is seen to be inside ourselves that we attain bliss and reality: *tam ātmastam ye anupaśyanti dhīraḥ.* Now a further question crops up. If God is the first and only cause of the world, does it not mean that He is the one material and instrumental cause of the world? Is He not the shaper as well as the matter out of which the world is shaped? If indeed it is God out of which the universe has come and that too by his instrumentality, is not the universe but only a mode, a manifestation or a form of the one God who is without a second? The Upaniṣads say that it is so. If indeed only one God without a second was before the beginning of the world, the world must have naturally come forth from

Him only. So the whole universe is but He Himself: *sat eva saumya edam agre āsīt; ekam eva advitīyam.* The gold ornaments which once were solid gold before they were chiselled and shaped so, and which will become solid gold if they are but melted, cannot be considered as anything but gold. So also the world, that arises or emerges out of God and dissolves in Him again, is but God. Thus God is to be considered as *viśva-mūrti* and *viśva-rūpa.* Beautiful is the prayer in the *Bhagavad-Gītā* to this: God who is the All; our adorations unto thee, O All, from all sides, *namostu te sarvataḥ eva sarva.* Thus God is not only the supreme presiding force of all things, but He is also the all-pervading omnipresent being, nay, He is the All: *sarvam khalu idam brahmā, na iha nānā asti kiñcana.* Then not only the trees and forests, the books and the tables, but men and women are also the Divine. Thus when we reach the highest pinnacles of true theism, we see the same Absolute. The Hari of the devotees is the *Brahman* of the philosophers. When we attain this vision we become indifferent as to how the Absolute is called. We no longer argue whether it is Kālī or Kṛṣṇa, Allāh or the Buddha. The impersonal formless Absolute is worshipped by the frail heart of man as the tender and kind deity. Rigorously logical minds alone can revel in the Absolute. All of us cannot become either Bradley or Śaṅkara. So the vastness of the universal spirit, when drawn on the canvas of mind, takes shape and becomes the personal God. The Upaniṣads and the *Bhagavad-Gītā* therefore indiscriminately called the Absolute as He or It. If the Nāyanārs could picture Him as Śiva and could see His eternal *tāṇḍava* dance in the motions of the planets, the movements of the machines and the throbbing of the heart, all credit unto them. If the Āḷwars could imagine Him as Viṣṇu and could see only the hurling of His *sudarśana* discus in the wars of the world, the shaping of history and the destinies of man, our hats off unto them. If the *ṛṣi* of the Upaniṣads could see the *Brahman* before him and behind him, to his east and to his west, south and north, our salutations unto him: *brahma eva idam amṛtam purastāt; brahma paścād, brahma dakṣiṇātaḥ ca uttarāśca.* But we have to remember that the "Infinite" is not comprehended adequately even by the profoundest thoughts of the thinker or the warmest emotions of the devotee and that it cannot be described through words adequately. We have to at last confess as did one of the foremost mystics, Sri Aurobindo:

> Beyond the last pinnacle seized by the thinker
> He is crowned in His seats that for ever endure.

Another thing that has to be remembered is that the universe does not exhaust the Divine. The Divine has not only embraced, filled and saturated the universe to the brim, but is actually overflowing it. The Infinite has not completed or exhausted itself in the world. It transcends it. As the Puruṣasūkta metaphorically says, by one foot of His the whole universe has been measured: *sa bhūmim viśvatovṛta atyatistat daśāṅgulam*. Pantheism is not the full truth. The universe as it appears to us is only one of the million possibilities of the Divine. It is not the Divine in full. The Divine is unlimited, as such the universe, to repeat again, is not only full of it and saturated by it, but is also overflowing with it.

Third: We shall now see how the Upaniṣads arrive at the same conclusion through a psychological approach. Untutored man thinks that the eye, the leg or the arm is himself. But acute reflection shows us that these are all but accidental adjuncts in which the self clothes itself. The self is the innermost existence within us, which has the psycho-physiological elements as its vestures. I can best illustrate how the conception of self-conscious Being was arrived at in the Upaniṣads by narrating the story of Indra and Prajāpati, which is found in the *Chāndogya Upaniṣad.* It appears that Indra went to Prajāpati for instruction in the "science of self." Prajāpati first gave the general description of the self thus: "That which is free from sin and senility, from death and grief, from hunger and thirst and which imagines and desires nothing is the self." Prajāpati however wanted that Indra should discover the self himself; so when he was requested to denote the self, he replied that the self is that which is seen when one looks into a pail of water. That, he added, is the immortal *Brahman.* Having bathed and dressed very trim, Indra looked into the water. He saw his own body therein. He reflected and was as a result perplexed, "I say, this self in the water is well dressed when the body is well dressed, is fresh when the body looks fresh. If so, will it not be lame when the body is lame, crippled when the body is crippled and will it not also perish when the body perishes?" So Indra thought that this cannot be the self which was defined by Prajāpati and conveyed him his doubts. Then Prajāpati said, "The immortal self is he who moves about happy in dreams." Indra meditated upon this and found it to be also unsatisfactory, "Does one not feel as if he is struck or chased in dreams? Does one not feel pain or shed tears in dreams? Can that be the self?" When Indra went and showed this difficulty, Prajāpati replied, "The self is that which is at perfect rest and repose in dreamless-deep-sleep." Indra considered this reply and found it to be very much wanting. He expressed his objection to Prajāpati, "In dreamless-deep-sleep, the self knows not that he is, nor is he aware of anything that exists. He is indeed destroyed and annihilated. How can that be the real self?" Then answered Prajāpati finally, "O Indra, this body is subject to death, but it is at the same time the container of the eternal self. In fact, the self is free from pain and pleasure. Only when he associates himself with the body, he experiences pain and pleasure. He is neither the nose nor the eye. He is the person of the nose — the knower who smells; the nose is but an instrument of smelling. As lightning and thunder which are formless appear in their own form, so too the self appears in his own form. This being who appears in his own form is the supreme Person."

The moral of this parable is this: The self of man is the true subject, it is never the object. It is that which sees and not that which is seen. It cannot be the arithmetical sum of all the qualities which are called "me." It is that which stands supreme beyond and behind all these qualities. So the body which is born and which is susceptible to growth, decay and death is not the self. Nor can it be the dreaming or thinking subject. Though dream consciousness is not dependant on the body and as such is free from suffering and allied imperfections, it still changes every moment. As Indra has pointed out it is still the empirical self; and as such has a fixed locus in space and time. It is a mere series of fleeting mental states. So it is not the indestructible permanent self. Objects of experience require a permanent subject. Moreover there cannot be an object without a subject, though a subject can exist without an object. The self therefore is the fundamental thing, the basis of everything else. All mental activities — feelings, conations, wills and imaginations — in short, all experience points towards a central reality; the self. So even when waking and dreaming are absent, the continuance of consciousness is to be recognized. Otherwise how is Rāma still the same Rāma after a sound sleep? So in deep sleep too, the self exists though it contemplates on nothing. But what is the nature of this self? We say that consciousness exists in sleep. But how can consciousness exist without being conscious of? As Berkeley has said, "to say that mind exists without thinking is a contradiction, nonsense, nothing." Can fire be without burning something? So also can there be a self, without being aware of something? As Lao Tzu has queried, "if the soul in a perfectly dreamless sleep thinks, feels and wills nothing, is the soul then at all, and if it is, how is it?" Indra says: "There is in that case no soul. It is annihilated." Thus the Upaniṣad sounds the death knell of pure subjectivism. The self is not therefore a bare abstraction. It is the true whole. It is the subject which is the ground of all experience. It is the real of which both the dream and waking experiences are only inadequate presentations. It is the identity that runs through all the differences. But thereby it is not meant that it is the mere negation of them. It is the one dynamic universal consciousness, which embraces all the varied distinctions. It is the permanent subject which persists in waking, dreaming and sleep too. All our awareness, in other words all the varied states of consciousness and all the facts of nature are based on it. It is the central light which illumines everything. If it is not there everything else vanishes. For without the percipient how can there be the perceived? Without that self there cannot be any knowledge or memory; and where knowledge is absent can there be a known? Therefore it is the universal ground of all objects. It is the subject and hence the sustainer of objects. To be brief, it is the universal subject and also the universal object. It is that which sees and sees not. This fundamental identity of the subject and the object, this reality of a universal consciousness is the *ātman*. It is that supreme reality where the individual coincides with the central principle. It is the highest fruition, *ānanda* where knower, known and knowledge become one. *Ātman* is *ānandamaya*. It is positive bliss, dynamic enjoyment, and conscious beatitude. It includes all, all things flow from it. It is the transcendent bliss where the distinctions of knower and known cease, and fuse into one. But it is not mere abstraction, not a nothing. In fact, it is the most concrete.

It is concretion itself. It is not a blank, but this ideal reality cannot be described adequately through words or grasped in full by the mind. Because, how can the knower be known or the light be lighted? But simply because it is impossible to be adequately comprehended, it is not non-existent. It is as the *Kena Upaniṣad* says, that which makes mind think but cannot in turn be thought of by the mind. If at all it has to be described it is to be described as the highest integral fruition, *ānanda.* However if we want to go beyond mere comprehension and wish to realize it, we can do so only when we can identify ourselves with it. Only when we become the All, we can know the All. When we do that all our doubts will be resolved, our fears will be shattered and we enjoy the eternal bliss: *abhayam amr̥tam vindati, ānandam aśnāti.* We attain then the exuberance of life (*praṇāraṇam*), beatitude of mind (*mana ānandam*) and fullness of peace (*śānti samr̥ddham*).

As no religion can be understood without knowledge of its cardinal tenets, Hinduism could not be understood without the basic doctrines of Vedānta.

4

Religion in Life

RELIGION on the practical side is righteous living, and is the practice of *dharma*, which means the inner law of one's own being. Conformity to the law of one's being, adherence to one's essential nature constitutes the practice of religion.

Hinduism never asks us to separate the other aspects of life from religion. No doubt man has several desires or cravings. The sex and parental instincts, the love of wealth and power and the craving for communion with the infinite, are all present simultaneously in the individual. But these desires, instincts, cravings or activities — whatever they might be called — never function in isolation. They act and react upon each other; crossing and re-crossing each other, modify and sometimes supplant one another. There is in all normal men and women, an interdependent co-ordination amongst them. Otherwise neurotic or dissociated personalities are produced. Man is a whole, and life is a totality. As such, all our desires and activities should be co-ordinated and integrated harmoniously. Those politicians and statesmen, who advise us to isolate religion from everyday politico-social life, do not know this fundamental psychological truth. No activity of man can be separated from his other activities. If at all one functions, one can function as a whole. If the contrary is seen in anyone, he is either a black-guard or a mal-adjusted person. There are preachers and so-called spiritualists, who warn us to keep away from life and politics. People who imagine that a truly religious man ought to be an acolyte of asceticism or a votary of life-negation are harbouring the most colossal of delusions. Real religion and sincere spiritualism consist in the perception and unflinching adoration of truth and infinity. Truth is never narcotic, it is dynamic. Infinity excludes nothing, it embraces all. As such a true religious man does not alienate himself from anything that is of interest to humanity. In the words of Terence, he would be able to say: "I am a man; nothing pertaining to humanity is alien to me."

Religion shows men how to live, a richer and fuller life. If it could not do that, in other words, if it cannot be of any practical use, then who owns a religion. If religion is merely to alienate us from the suffering world, if it is merely to make us lose our sanity by dipping us into depths of unintelligibility masquerading under profundity of spiritual truth, if it is merely to ignore the tremendous assets of science and revel in the hallucinations of fancied heaven and angelic hosts, if it is merely to construct systems of reflection without any reference to the primary and empirical facts of the world and life, if it is merely to make us adopt superstitious silliness and orthodox foolishness and if it is merely to cry halt in the name of God to every novel innovation and every new step in the ladder of human progress then, I am afraid, no sane man can be religious. If that is religion, the sooner we shake ourselves from its shackles the better.

But fortunately religion is not that. It is meant to serve practical ends. It does not end in abstraction and nothingness; it ends in action. It embraces an individual and through him the society and race; and not only contributes to the welfare of these but also makes itself felt in living history. The role of religion does not stop with showing men what they are; it also shows them how to shape the course of life in the light of what they are. Men, say the Upaniṣads, are the sons of nectar: *amṛtasya putraḥ*. Their root is bliss and the infinite; their fruit shall be bliss and the infinite. Can the root and the fruit be the same and yet the stem is dissimilar? If it is so, it is a monstrosity, not a normality. "You emanate from the Divine, you will again inevitably be merged in the Divine; your nature is essentially Divine. You are the Divine. So why not you act and also appear as the Divine." That is the message of religion to us.

Hinduism does not believe in a fundamental feud between the human world of instincts and the life of the spirit. The misapprehension that spiritual life is opposed to the worldly relationship, rests on the mistaken notion that the world is a phantom, a dream and a delusion or that the finite is opposed to the infinite. Just as it has been pointed out that intuition is not opposed to intellect, but supplements and completes it; what should clearly be grasped now is that the eternal is manifested in the temporal, the infinite is expressed in the finite and the Divine is embodied within the human. The Divine is fulfilling itself in the world. The world is not something which has to be eschewed, abandoned and renounced. If we do that we are after all discarding the Divine itself. The world is *līlā* or *krīḍā* or sport of God. It is the *līlā* of the Viṣṇu, the *tāṇḍava* of the Śiva. We should of course remember that the divine does not exhaust itself in the world. It stands towering over the Universe after having filled it. If we want to reach its dizzy heights, the way is not to renounce the world, but to utilize and transcend it. The way to reach the top storey is not the high jump, but the gradual ascending of the steps that lead to it. The temporal is the pathway to the eternal, the finite is the ladder for the infinite.

But here many relevant doubts do occur to us. What precisely is the meaning when it is said that we should be in the midst of the worldly forces but yet be unshaken by them?

The world, to be frank, means the raising of family and the earning of money. These in the very nature of them involve desires and attachments. But are these not the very essential things to be weeded out if one wants to lead the spiritual life? The solution that is often suggested is that we should live in the world, but be indifferent to it. We should sit quietly suffering unintruding, observing everything silently, without reacting to the external impacts. We should no doubt continue to exist, suicide is not the short-cut to heaven. But we should so exist, that we should not at all be active. We should merely be the passive and silent lookers-on. This is the stoic way. Probably it is what some religions advise us to do. But this is nothing but psychological escapism. If we are to conduct ourselves in the world as though we are not in the world, then is it not better to renounce the world with its civilization and go back to the caves and wilds where once our remote forefathers used to sojourn? Or better still, if spirituality consists in avoiding the world as far as possible, why not avoid it altogether?

This is not what Hinduism teaches us. The way to bliss neither lies in the abandonment of the world, nor in residing in the world without participating in its activities. We should not be in the world standing merely as witnesses. We should be the active doers. This was the advice, which was given on the battlefields of Kurukṣetra by Lord Kṛṣṇa. But how, the question arises, is to do this? What happens to our duties? We have so many duties to discharge? Life is almost a series of duties; and they are so diverse — duty to oneself, one's wife, one's children, one's country and so on infinitum. How can we discharge all these duties simultaneously? If we are loyal to our own self, we have to forsake sometimes the interests of our wife and child. If we want to be devoted to our country alone, we cannot be the votaries of humanity. So which are the duties that we ought to undertake? Which are those that we have to relinquish? The *Bhagavad-Gītā* is definite on this point: Life is a totality, there cannot be any compartmentalization of its duties. Take life as an integral whole and undertake and discharge that which is necessarily to be done: *kartavyam karma.* Consider everything you do as a sacrifice, *yajña,* unto the spirit; and do whatever it might be as simply something that has to be done.

The question that inevitably occurs is, how to determine which our duty (*kartavya*) is. What is that we should do necessarily? Have we to do everything that the ignorant do? The answer is of course in the negative. No doubt, all activity has its source ultimately in the Divine. Still the Divine sometimes expresses itself very indirectly and perversely. The sun, no doubt, shines on the dung-hill as well as on the grassy plain. But on that account we need not resort to the dung-hill for basking in the sunshine. There are activities which are essentially of the earth, earthly. The animal instincts and the brute urges have no place in the spiritual scheme. But these on that account do not constitute any serious hindrance. As soon as one turns to the Divine and develops unattachment towards the fruits of one's actions, these obstacles disappear ipso facto: *kṣipram bhavati dharmātmā.* As soon as the fire is kindled within, all the past and the present will be burnt away: *jñānāgniḥ sarva karmāni bhasmasāt kurute.* The slate will be wiped clean and we almost start with a fresh one. Our environment will be transformed. Then we will look not only through a new pair of eyes, but almost feel that we are born new. This is what is meant by *dvija,* the twice-born.

This is the message of Hinduism. Intense dynamic activity with its locus in the calm unsettled silent bliss of the spirit, is what it urges us to adopt. It does not ask us to leave the ploughs and the fields, the cities and the cinemas, the classes and the colleges, the machines and the factories, the streets and the markets. It wants us to remain amidst all these, but calm and unruffled. But this does not mean that we should merely be the silent spectators of the show, without active participation. Hinduism asks us to take our full share in the struggles and aspirations, the toils and turmoils of humanity. There is no use of our continuing to be in the world without taking any interest in it. We should not be living-corpses, *jīvanmṛtas*. We should be intensely active taking part in all the movements of the world; for is not the world the sport, the *līlā*, of the Divine? But while doing anything our aim should be nothing that is of the earth. We should feel that all our works are sacrifices, *yajñas*, to the Divine; and should therefore have no attachment to the fruits thereof, *niṣkāma karma*. It is thus that religion has to be applied to daily living. Only when the tenets of religion have permeated and sunk deep into the very marrow of our bones, we can be said to be truly religious. Religion keeps before us the central truth of all existence, the sheet anchor of all life, and if we but take refuge in it, it will never tolerate either the egoistic veils or the emotional distortions of our inner light. Whatever we might be, we need the sure guidance and secure sailing of our life's ship; and the only thing that can give us this guarantee is religion. The value of religion lies in the practical direction it gives to day-to-day life. The connection between the home, the farm, the factory, the office and the theatre with religion is now evident and plain. Religion is living right. Its final object is to tell us — how to transform our being and how to transform the colourless and mechanical life of ours into the richer, fuller and joyous life of the spirit.

The first and foremost duty of spiritual life is sincerity. If there is really an idea of leading a spiritual life, we should want to do so most sincerely. Of course, if one has felt the vital urge to remould his life, if one has caught a glimpse of the glow of the Divine, he is but following the call of his being. As such, as soon as one has realized the insufficiency and inadequacy of his mundane life he would also realize that nothing less than the Infinite can satisfy him. With this step one automatically becomes sincere. He will be aware then of the weaknesses and imperfections inherent in himself, the obstacles and barriers that have to be crossed and the habits and outlook that have to be cultivated. But all this will only be mental. Only when this awareness of the destiny of man and the path to it assumes a concrete form and moulds life and character, one can be said to be truly sincere. If one knows and comprehends but yet does not act upon it, he is playing a double game. Mere inner perception, bare intellectual grasp of the Divine is not enough. Our sincerity is known only when the flesh is ready to obey the law of the spirit.

If our inner convictions point to one way and if our body follows an alien path, it means that true harmony has not been achieved. The discord is still there, the sounds have not yet become a tune. The immediacy, the urgency and the vitality of one's sincere craving for the spiritual life can be known only when it influences the body. When the body is entirely in the grips of the innermost being within us, when it ruthlessly and inevitably executes everything in accordance with the dictates of the voice within, then we can be treated to be truly sincere. Our life then will be blended in a harmony that surprises us, our heart will beat with the rhythm of the Divine, and our actions will echo the depths of the infinite. When we are thus following the inner law of the spirit we need not follow any other law. We become the law ourselves. We need no other light to illuminate us. We become the lights. Christ and Kr̥ṣṇa broke the law many a time. But what they violated was only man-made law, the conventions of the land. At the same time they were following a higher law, the *ṛta*, the law immanent in all beings. Such people need not look after something extraneous for the guidance of their actions. For why should one look for the prototype, when one has himself become the archetype? And the path they have followed and the directions they have given are the law — the commandments — only unto us, we cannot discover the law for ourselves. When we achieve that stage, we too need not look outside ourselves for guidance. We might, secure and steadfast, follow the dictates of our own being. For, is not it the same being, the same essence that is in all? Hence we will necessarily be in the right, because we then become the manifestations of the Right. Thus in the final stages, just as intellect remains far behind the level of intuition, religion transcends morality. He who has attained the highest is above all laws; for he is the law himself. When thus once the soul attains the real and eternal, the human body becomes suffused with the radiance of divinity and in that all that is vile and all that is mean will simply be burnt up. In that stage, it will no more be the individual self, the ego that does anything. His will becomes God's will and God's will becomes his. He has merged himself in the whole and has become the whole, for the ego has fused itself in the super-ego. Law then fulfils itself in love. Those who have achieved this cannot do anything evil. The saint's activity will spontaneously be saintly. He becomes a law unto himself, he is *svatantrāt*. All of us have within us the capacity and the possibility to rise to this full divine stature. If the striving and the sincerity are there, the possibility of becoming one with the Divine, God, is not a remote one. It can be realized here and now.

But as many of us have not yet ascended those dizzy heights, and since long is the journey and the path difficult — and certain though it is that we will one day arrive at the summit, still in the interim period we need not be rudderless. Meanwhile we have to tread the path that has been trodden by the wise among the ancients. We have to drive along the road that has been driven past by the knower of truth, devoted to duty.

> *mahājano yena gataḥ sa panthaḥ* — *Mahābhārata*
>
> *ye tatra brāhmanaḥ sama dharśinaḥ dharma kāmasyuḥ yathā te tesu varteran tathā tesu vartethaḥ* । *eṣa ādeśaḥ* ॥
>
> — *Taittirīya Upaniṣad*

Hence arises the need for us to follow the laws of the land and the customs of society, till we are able to discover the law ourselves. But society is not something that remains static. It changes with the progress of time. That which was a wholesome custom or a healthy institution at one time ceases to remain so with the change in times. *Dharma* therefore, changes with every *yuga* (age) and every *deśa* (country). What might have been to the best interests of our forefathers cannot be so to ours. The institution of caste is an instance in point. There are some who, swayed by emotions, attribute the authorship of caste system to a few wicked priests, who wanted to oppress society and ride it rough-shod. An impartial study of the genesis and growth of the caste system shows that it was not the intention of its inaugurators to perpetrate inequalities and fascist tendencies. It started at first as a social organization of different racial types. It was intended as a solution to the problem of racial conflicts. Victorious races often weed out or exterminate the vanquished races. This was the fate which fell to the lot of the Red Indians, and the Bushmen of the Pacific islands. The Europeans in the pride of their own culture and strength ruthlessly massacred and blotted them out. No doubt compared with the European adventurers, the Red Indians were in a state of barbarity. But if they had been allowed to survive and if they had been given the chances to progress, probably by now they would have taken their place amongst the other great nations of the world. But they were not destined to do so. Their blood flowed in streams and made the plains of America more fertile for the Europeans.

The Vedic Aryans did not wish to follow this annihilation policy towards the alien races. Neither did they want to humiliate, enslave and subordinate their vanquished races. In the name of superior culture and civilization, they did not act, as do the ruling races of the present day in South Africa and in some of the American states like Georgia; and so the Vedic Aryans rightly chose the one remaining alternative of assimilation and reform. Whole hosts of primitive hordes were absorbed into the Hindu fold. All the absorbed tribes were reformed, civilized and yet at the same time were treated as one of the family. Writes Jackson in the *Indian Antiquary*:

> Those Indians indeed have a poor opinion of their country's greatness, who do not realize how it has tamed and civilized the nomads of Central Asia, so that wild Turcoman tribes have been transformed into some of the most famous of the Rājpūt royal races.

But the absorbed aboriginal races were not asked to surrender their individuality. They were allowed not only to modify themselves but also the Hindu system. The good that was in their own indigenous customs and culture was incorporated into the Aryan and thus there emerged from these heterogeneous races and their discordant beliefs, a different, comprehensive and sublime culture which retained the good of all component groups. Each one of these exclusive groups, representing a distinct type, formed a different caste; and as time moved on, the number of castes began to increase with the increase in the number of races absorbed. But there was no oppression of one caste by another. Each realized that it was but an individual unit of the harmonious whole. They were bound together by common interests and held together by a common code of ethics; and so with the march of time the process of welding together became so intense, that the several component castes became mutual complementaries. But interbreeding between the different castes was discouraged. Each racial stock was encouraged to keep its distinctness and its heritage separate. They were not allowed to fuse together. It was this that proved to be the bane of the caste system.

Very soon after the rise of the caste system, confusion between the racial and the vocational began to confound it. Castes came to mean the various strata of society. Caste which was formulated for preserving the distinctness of the different racial stocks, began to operate towards the rigid separation of different occupational groups. The *ṛṣi*s of ancient times were farmers and warriors. They tilled the land at times of peace and took to the sword at times of emergency. But this healthy state of affairs was not allowed to last long. Complexes of inferiority and superiority gradually manifested themselves. Vocation became strictly hereditary. The son of the priest was asked to continue as a priest though he had the aptitude for things military. The son of the peasant was forced to remain a peasant, though he was fit to be the leader of society. Rules of inter-marriage grew stricter and stricter. Those who violated these rules were severely punished. But still not all the rules could stop the flow of blood from the *cāṇḍāla* to the brāhmin and from the brāhmin to the *cāṇḍāla*. The progeny of these prohibited marriages were treated as sinners and untouchables, niṣādas and kirātas. Gradually the social barriers between these vocational groups grew rigid. The talented sons of the humble farmers and peasants were denied the opportunities to rise to the top. The incompetent offspring of the priests and warriors were allowed to dominate and oppress the others. Rivalry, jealousy and rebellion grew. The Buddhist and Jaina movements were partial reactions against this unsatisfactory state of affairs; and in the end the *Bhagavad-Gītā* had to declare that "the divisions of caste depend upon one's character and action" and not on birth: *guṇa karma vibhāgasaḥ*. Thus the idea of the divine supremacy of one caste over another was flouted. The advent of Islam with its belief in the brotherhood of humanity and the purgatory and reformatory zeal of Vemana and Basava in the south and Rāmānanda and Kabīr in the north have done much towards the elimination of this social evil which has sapped the energy of Hinduism for the past hundreds of years. The institution of caste which once came into being for the good of society has now to be broken down for the good of society. Radhakrishnan says: "It has now degenerated into an instrument of oppression and intolerance, it tends to perpetuate inequality and develop the spirit of exclusiveness. . . ." But it is, of course, hard for the vested interests to give up their false notions of superiority and prestige and mingle with the downtrodden and the oppressed. As the religious head of the Śṛṅgerī Pīṭha has observed: "The sub-divisions which originated for stabilizing and preserving the community have now become a source of weakness." And the sooner this cancer of the Hindu Society is removed, the better. As the greatest Hindu, Mahatma Gandhi declared: "If Hinduism is to survive, it would have to be casteless." — February I2, 1947.

Hinduism is often called the *varṇāśrama dharma* i.e. the *dharma* based upon *varṇa* (caste) and *āśrama* (life-stage). The Hindu sages divided the life-period of an individual into four successive stages. Man is made up of so many desires, instincts and impulses. If all these have to be allowed to play their role in one's life without giving rise to any discordance, they have to be worked out into a harmonious pattern. The division of life into the four *āśrama*s of *brahmacarya, gṛhastha, vānaprastha* and *saṁnyāsa* suggests a scheme towards this solution. Life's journey should also have its halts. It need not be post-haste rushing past at a bewildering speed. We can enjoy a journey only when we stop regularly at the wayside inns, and mix with the people and see the land around. Otherwise in vain would be the journey, if we go at a non-stop speed. Rolling stones gather no mass. The four *āśrama*s provide the caravansarais for our life's journey. The first stage is *brahmacarya,* the period of discipline, study and training. The future citizen of the world is taught the way to lead his life, in this stage. The student is required to reside for a definite period in the house of the teacher. Thus opportunities for coming into intimate contact with the teacher and imbibing sound habits and culture from the repositories of wisdom were provided. The teachers and students used to live together, eat together and work together, *sahanāvavatu, sahanau bhunaktu.* Thus not only the students were instructed in the arts and sciences, but were also taught the art of living. The high ideals of simple living and high thinking were inculcated alongside with the everyday lessons. Habits of truth-speaking, non-violence, respect to elders and adherence to one's own culture and pride in one's heritage were promoted by the living contact of the teachers with the students. They lived as one family and worked towards one ideal. Anyone who has read Newman's University Sketches can see that it was towards establishing this ideal that he strove. The salvation of India lies in our universities adopting this ancient ideal and method of education, again. Only when our universities aim at producing good citizens who can lead their lives aright without any complexes, inhibitions and prejudices, the present state of affairs can be mended. It was with this aim that Tagore established the Visvabharati; and it is our good fortune that it is receiving increasing importance and encouragement, due to the formation of the national Government. But one such institution is not sufficient. We need scores of such institutions to lift us to our former glory. We would do well to remember that "right education is that which liberates us" *sa vidyā ya muktaye* from our prejudices, poverty and slavery and takes us into ever-widening regions of freedom and love.

Gṛhastha is the next stage in life. A human being, be it man or woman, requires a life companion. One cannot face alone the troubles and tasks of the *saṁsāra.* Moreover natural impulses, the instincts of sex and reproduction, should have their outlets. There is no use of repressing these instincts. Again and again they raise their heads and if they are forcibly suppressed they act in other ways; and then, there is nothing guilty or specially demoniacal about sex. It is just one more appetite like thirst and hunger. As such it need not be curbed. But just as our being thirsty cannot justify our drinking from any pond or ditch, the inelegant and unceremonious venting of sex passion in any possible way is to be reprehended. Restraint is as much necessary here as in eating and drinking. So the Hindu *śāstra*s encourage marriage as a rule. It is not only necessary for an expression of our normal impulses, but it also aids us in the development of personality. Marriage is not the culmination of our life. It is the beginning of a new and more glorious chapter in our life. It has not only an individual but a social aspect. It fulfils not only the *kāma* but the *dharma.* Its aim is not only the whetting of our instincts, but the propagation of our race. We should strive to produce amongst us heroes, and true men. "May we have great heroes amongst us," is the Vedic prayer: *suvīraso bhavema.* This other aspect of marriage ennobles the otherwise purely sensual affair. The perfect marriage is the truly monogamous marriage. The ideals of Sītā-Rāma, Candramatī-Hariścandra, Sāvitrī-Satyavān, Madālasā-Alarka, are those which are to be kept in mind by every Hindu couple. Marriage is meant to make the husband and wife life companions through thick and thin. Neither need tyrannize over the other. Both have to subordinate their individual tastes and tempers for the sake of a harmonious ideal. Both have to put up with so much that may not be liked. But they should try to make the marriage a successful consummation and not a mutual misunderstanding. Hinduism generally discourages divorce. Neither has the husband the right to desert his wife, nor the wife has the liberty to forsake her husband. No doubt divergences in opinion and conduct give rise to discomfort. But these momentary feelings or fancies should not give rise to a disruption of the alliance with one's chosen companion. Only in poetry and fiction, we find a couple who can agree with each other in everything. However deliberate and advised one's choice of a companion be much depends upon chance and charm. Individual peculiarities and idiosyncrasies unexpectedly crop up. That does not mean that we should shake hands and say, "good-bye, cheerio." That is neither heroism nor saintly. The lack of agreement between husband and wife should be an incentive for a better understanding of each other's viewpoint. If agreement at home is rare, there is no sense in talking of a world-federation and brotherhood of men. There are critics who say that one should not lose one's individuality and stunt one's self-development, for making marriage a success. They are labouring under a grievous error. Marriage is precisely meant for killing one's egoistic self. Man is essentially a social animal; and he who cannot sacrifice just a part of his ego for his life-mate, is he not to be reckoned as one of the pests of society? Such being the case, Hinduism strictly abhors the dissolution of a marriage. Divorce is not a heroic deed. The woman who changes her husband as often as she changes her blouse is not a phenomenon to be adored; nor is it really wonderful or romantic if a man who is sick of his wife takes to another. To do such things is something which is awfully common, nay, chaotically brutal. To divorce is to confess failure, to show the world that one is a misfit for marriage. Such people ought to be psychoanalysed and cured of their inhibitions and maladjustments. The debauchers and the prostitutes, psychology tells us, are the feeble-minded and the imbeciles. Real romance and true heroism consists in clinging to one's wife or husband through good report and bad, through prosperity and adversity and in health and sickness.

Dreams of world-state and fraternity of humanity will concretise much quicker if everyone endeavours to follow this ideal of marriage, which Hinduism holds out. Marriage is not mere carnal companionship, but spiritual partnership. It is meant to serve a higher end. It is not either for sensual enjoyment or for vegetative reproduction. Through it, one attains one's full stature. It forms the unit of the society, the city and the country. True civilization starts at home. It is the preparatory preamble for things higher. As such it should not be considered a cheap commercial or sexual alliance. Married life or *gṛhastha*, should be considered as a sacrifice, *yajña*, to the spirit. It is most auspicious, *maṅgalam*, and holy, *pavitram.*

The third stage in life is *vānaprastha.* Man is not born to serve the ends of his own family and society for ever. He cannot end as the servant of his family or community. The Infinite within cannot be attained in these alone. A stage comes when we should turn our attention to things higher than our home and children. In the twilight of life, after hairs have turned white and chins have doubled and wrinkles have formed one should resort to the seclusion of a retired life along with his wife, which is *vānaprastha.* In our life, a stage necessarily arrives when no longer can social duties and relations have a meaning for us. There is no use in forcing ourselves to do these unattached. We have to sacrifice them for the sake of the Divine. We should have to give up the show and completely devote ourselves to the Divine.

Here comes the last stage where the individual has completely shaken off his egoistic veils and has attained complete freedom. He becomes steadfast, *sthita-prajña*, and steady minded, *sthita-dhīḥ*. He will neither be elated by success nor tempted by wealth. He will neither be depressed by failure nor aggrieved by poverty. He will be free from ambition and attachment, from love and lust and from passion and penalty. He develops a spirit of equanimity. The whole world becomes his family. He lives in love and walks in truth. The Indian and the Chinese, the Russian and the French, the Negro and the American, are all equal in his eyes. He lives the true life of the spirit.

But it should be clearly understood that a real *saṁnyāsin*, never is indifferent to the world's welfare. He does not renounce the world and just walk away into the snows of the Himalayas or the wilds of the Vindhyas. His dearest ideal will be the upliftment of humanity to the heights he has ascended. As Medhātithi says, his renunciation is the surrendering of the notions of I and mine: *ahaṁkāra mamakāra tyāga eva saṁnyāsaḥ*. The true *saṁnyāsin* is never a social or anti-social. He is neither a useless appendage nor a mere ornament. Often he is considered to be a superfluity or a parasite of society. It is true that he cannot be loyal to the family, the group, the church or the country. He can be loyal to the spirit alone, but the spirit is the All. So his loyalty to the whole often is mistaken by the ordinary as anti-social or anti-patriotic. But never are the interests of humanity and the welfare of the world foreign to his heart. He will be always ready to serve the world. Did not Śiva, the greatest of our *saṁnyāsins*, gladly and willingly drink poison for saving the world? Did not Agastya, the foremost of sages, traverse the whole length of India accompanied by his wife, for spreading the Hindu culture? Coming to recent times did not the Buddha wander on foot from village to village to alleviate the sufferings of mankind and spread his simple, but ennobling message of *satya* and *ahiṁsā*. These are the typical ascetics, the true sages. No doubt the real *saṁnyāsins* have been few and rare. But it is they who truly represent the soul of India. So long as India followed their lead, it held its head high. Because, then it was following its own aptitude and tendency and carving itself in its own peculiar way. But the serene flow of the course of its life has been disturbed. India has been forcibly enslaved and brutally raped. This has enraged it and made it come out of its swoon. It is rediscovering itself. It has risen and will now not stand still. It will now march with unimpeded step and uncontrollable speed. It has a message to give to the world and a destiny of herself to fulfil. As Britain's Foreign Minister has said, India holds the key to the present world situation. "If that key can be held in security and peace then the peace of the world can be held for hundreds of years."

The potentialities of the Divine are within the human. Man encases the Divine within himself. He has only to pierce the sheaths that veil the Infinite within, and allow it to radiate its light and to the whole world. But for this he need not resort to any mysterious processes. The only thing that is required is sincerity to the core and faith in himself. To achieve this he needs to be truly moral; and true morality consists in being true to one's own being, in following the dictates of one's inner voice. Meanwhile adherence to one's *dharma* and ordinary ethical canons provides the sure and secure path for entering this true life, the life of the spirit.

Part II
The Evolution of Hinduism

Hinduism, as a faith, is amorphous, many-sided, all things to all men. It is hardly possible to define it, or indeed to say definitely whether it is a religion or not, in the usual sense of the word. In its present form, and even in the past, it embraces many beliefs and practices, from the highest to the lowest, often opposed to and contradictory to each other.

— Jawaharlal Nehru

1

Draviḍian and Aryan Synthesis

In between 5000 and 6000 BC, while men were settling down to agriculture and forming the city states in Mesopotamia and the Nile Valley, there flourished a people in the Indus Valley who had a most remarkable and highly developed civilization. The impressive remains of this civilization in Mohen-jo-dāro and Harappā reveal to us, in the words of John Marshall, "an age-old civilization with many millennia of human endeavour behind it." Then came the Aryans in successive waves from the north-west. The first great cultural synthesis and fusion took place between the incoming Aryans, and the Draviḍians who were the representatives of the Indus Valley civilization.

Till recently books of history used to tell us that the Aryans were the earliest invaders of India and before whom this country was barbarous and uncivilized. There were invaders even before the Aryans, but they all settled down and evolved a culture which astonishes modern scholars by its extent and depth. No doubt the Aryans first appeared on the scene as the victors, but they were soon absorbed in the ranks of the vanquished. At first of course there was much hatred and resentment between the newcomers and the old occupants. But gradually it wore away. The Draviḍians in course of time forgot that they were people with a much older civilization than the newcomers. On the other hand the Aryans too lost gradually their disdain and distrust for the culture of the

Draviḍians, as they came into more intimate contact with it day by day. Soon they settled down and took things for granted. This gave birth to a new and organic way of life; and out of this synthesis and fusion grew the Indian culture, with distinctive elements of both. The Aryans and Draviḍians worked together and there emerged from this conjoint endeavour, a distinct cultural pattern of life and thought — Hinduism. But it did not retain any heterogeneity at all; the different threads were so subtly and dexterously woven, that the separate strands and diverse colours went to make a most beautiful fabric.

The Aryo-Draviḍian struggles for supremacy thus ended in a synthesis which heralded a new stage of achievement in the human progress. It was at this time that caste arose. It was a device which enabled the different races to live together in harmony. It was based, as has already been pointed out, on the differences in race and later in function. The system was a very fluid one. Not only were Draviḍian gods accepted in the pantheon of the Aryans, but Draviḍian priests were accepted as brāhmins. Migration from one caste into another was common. Gradually it lost its elasticity and became rigid. In course of time it came to be based on birth. But this was an unforeseen calamity. But even now India understands what caste means. The fact that Gandhi, who is not a brāhmin by birth has become the supreme leader of India with the magnetic power to move millions of hearts, shows that India has a true understanding of the institution of caste.

Thus the civilization of Mohen-jo-dāro was not destroyed, but it was taken up and assimilated by the Aryans, and on its foundations was built the future Hindu culture. Śiva with the trident is none other than the terrible Rudra of the Aryans fused with the pre-Aryan conception of a hill-god, Girīśa. The phallic worship which was associated with him was also accepted and insisted upon. The story which tells us that Śiva was refused admission to the sacrificial feast of Dakṣa, shows that some conservative Aryans had at first objections to his worship. The conception of Viṣṇu as a blue-dark god, also points towards his un-Aryan origin. Similarly the story which narrates that Kṛṣṇa fought with Indra, on the banks of Aṁsumatī, shows that he too was a Draviḍian god who was taken up by Aryans and worshipped. This indiscriminate worship of any god, tree or mountain, led to the recognition that reality is one and unified and that its manifestations are different to different persons. It was discovered, quite early in the history of Hinduism and a remarkable discovery it was for that age, that every creed contains some elements of truth within it and that it shows the depth of man's insight at different stages into the same truth about the same reality. It is generally held that the Vedas are books full of obnoxious rituals and worship of different phenomena of nature. But this is far from the truth. The earliest religious experiences as recorded in the *Ṛgveda* pay little heed to form and ritual. No doubt divinity was attributed to every element and force of nature. They, looking at life with a vigorous imagination and an unsophisticated faith, woke up to a sense of inexhaustible mystery implicit in life. Writes Pandit Nehru: "Often, as I look at this world, I have a sense of mysteries, of unknown depths. The urge to understand it comes to me; to be in tune with it and to experience it in its fullness." This sense of the mysterious and the urge to understand it was there in those Vedic people. Their deepest yearnings were satisfied by a communion with the forces of nature. But they at the same time understood that all these phenomena of nature were but manifestations of the One Reality; and similarly the many gods were looked upon as multiple embodiments of the one Universal spirit.

The second profound discovery which the Vedic people made was that of the prevalence of an order throughout the universe. The regularity of the movements of the planets and the never-failing succession of the seasons, suggested to them that things followed a definite chalked-out course and that the world was not the blind fury of chaotic elements. The world was realized to be a universe and a cosmos. This cosmic order was called the *ṛta*.

2

Upaniṣadic Idealism

By the time this astonishing development in thought took place, the Aryans were settled down. A prosperous and notable civilization, with a mixture of the old and new, was the result. Caste came to mean the division of labour. Vocational differences in society ossified into caste. As a result of this, religion became degenerated and was monopolized by a particular class. This class regarded religion as their profession and means of livelihood. But religion, in its true sense, cannot be the exclusive monopoly of a particular individual or group of individuals. So the priestly class to justify its existence began to invent elaborate practices and impose them on the innocent multitude. Ritual grew and sacrifice developed. In course of time, the enormous emphasis on the empty and meaningless forms of rituals and worship made people forget the true spirit and inner meaning of religion. Completion of sacrifices was considered more important than the perfection of personality. Religion became mechanical, external and formalistic. Thinking minds and sensitive hearts grew discontented with this sort of religion. They found the necessity for a restatement of the old truth contained in the *sūkta*s of the *Ṛgveda* and a revival of the spirituality that lay embedded in them. Their efforts culminated in the Upaniṣads.

The Upaniṣads assert that salvation cannot be sought through sacrifice. Perfection ought to be spiritual. The experience of the oneness of oneself with the universe, the identity of the individual soul with the all, is the real practice of religion. Sacrifice does not mean the offering of ghee or rice or animals into the fire. The true sacrifice is man himself. The *yajña* is the *puruṣa.* The whole of life has to be made one sacrament to the spirit. "The morning oblation of the sacrifice consists in the first twenty-four years and true consecration consists in abstaining away from sensuous pleasures. The hymns are the spontaneous words of joy and laughter. The payments to be offered are truth and non-violence, generosity and purity; and death is the pacificator bath, *avabṛdha snāna*, at the end of sacrifice." That is the true sacrifice, says the *Chāndogya.* Thus the Upaniṣads disparage the utility of sacrifices and outer worship. They ask us to consider our whole life as a sacrifice to the Divine. But this is merely hinted in the Upaniṣads which was later developed in the *Bhagavad-Gītā.* They are more preoccupied with the nature of ultimate Reality. Their quest is for the true, the real in life. Dissatisfaction with things and second causes made them search for reality behind the world. They scorned the common sense view that empirical knowledge is the final knowledge. The ultimate reality if there is one, must be eternal and unchanging. But this infinite and imperishable truth cannot be grasped in its fullness by man's finite mind. At most it can grasp some small aspect of it limited by time and space and by the state of development of a particular mind. As intellect develops and enlarges its scope, new aspects and new horizons of truth come to light. But ritualistic religion tries to imprison truth in set forms and dogmas and encourages empty ceremonials and barren practices. No doubt rituals impress upon man the awe and mystery of the unknown that surrounds him, but they at the same time discourage him from understanding the depths of that unknown. It is precisely against this tendency that the

Upaniṣads revolt. They encourage a free spirit of enquiry and understanding into the mysterious and the unknown. The Upaniṣads are essentially movements which were intended to free the individual from the shackles of external authority and the bonds of excessive convention. Their creed is a pure spiritual doctrine. Their ritual is the contemplation of the Supreme that is beyond and within the world too. Their goal is the merging of the individual consciousness in the universal consciousness. Their meditation is on the plenitude of beauty and goodness. Their aim is the perception of the beauty, goodness and truth, *satyam śivam sundaram*, inherent everywhere. The establishment of a spiritual democracy was, in short, the ideal of the Upaniṣads. But this idealistic approach of the Upaniṣads did not make them blind to the world. They are not exclusively other-worldly. They did not preach the unreality and negation of the world. The world was conceived as the ultimate reality manifesting itself in manifold appearances. Similarly the various creeds were seen as the imperfect expressions of the one and the same truth. This attitude of the Upaniṣads, which is neither exclusively other-worldly nor solely worldly, developed a tolerant, synthetic and pervasive outlook and integrated Indian life into a unity, which recognizes all the differences as the diverse aspects of the one reality. It is this synthetic spirit of the Hindu thought which gave it a resilience and fluidity enabling it to resist and withstand all attempts to cut asunder the continuity and unity of the ancient tradition. The philosophy of the Upaniṣads forms the bedrock of the Hindu faith.

The very loftiness of the teaching of the Upaniṣads made it difficult to be understood by the populace. With the march of time the superstitious sacrificial religion again raised its head. The priestly class consolidated themselves and again became a power in the land. The rigours of the caste system and the irrational polytheism of the priests made the whole atmosphere choke with dry ceremonialism and empty formalism. Barren dogmas and petty creeds swayed the people. Exaggerated ritual and affected religion held the day. The scriptures attained an unexplainable sanctity. Regardless of the time and age, their injunctions came to be venerated as universally valid and applicable to all times. Morality, as a result of this, suffered. The letter of the Vedas instead of the spirit reigned. The thick fogs of metaphysical subtleties and theological conceits obscured the great truths of the Upaniṣads. Dialectical spiritualism and controversial speculation relegated the Upaniṣads to the background. The age was flooded with speculative chaos and ethical anarchy. Spiritualism was vulgarized and idealism was debased. Worships of the deities were accompanied by blood-curdling rites. Everyday a new god and a novel ghost were created. Rituals to invoke the blessings of these fancied creatures and avert their wrath, were invented. The relation between man and god became mechanical and commercial. The prevalence of a universal law, the *r̥ta,* was forgotten. The most sinful of actions and the most barbarous of crimes were committed. But they were deemed to be condoned as soon as one offered a goat to the god and a payment to the priest. The Upaniṣad conception of *yajña* was forgotten. *Tapas* came to mean self-mortification and soul-torture. Priests became prophets and magicians became mystics. In short there followed a period of disintegration and shaman religion after the Upaniṣads. This state of affairs could not satisfy even the masses in the long run. There arose the necessity for a reconstruction of the spirit. The need for popularizing the deep spiritual religion of the Upaniṣads, became imperative. There was the urgency for carrying the teachings of the Upaniṣad to the door of the common man in every village. In short, the lofty idealism of the Upaniṣads was soaring too high in the skies. There was the demand for bringing it down from its rarefied dizzy heights and making it the common property of the man in the street.

3

Voice of the Buddha

THIS need for a spiritual reconstruction and a moral resurrection crystallized in Kapilavastu. The idealism of the Upaniṣads was materialized in Gautama, the Buddha. The Buddha attacked superstition and priestcraft. He condemned metaphysical web-spinning and theological codifying. His appeal was to logic and his emphasis was on ethics. His whole teaching and method of approach came like the breath of the fresh breeze from the hills after the stale and putrefied air of ceremonial convention and metaphysical speculation. The Buddha's tremendous personality and his galvanic sincerity impressed the people enormously. Multitudes of men, women and children flocked to him as they did once again, six hundred years after, to hear Christ in Galilee. The Buddha and Christ constitute the two most outstanding personalities that have graced this earth. The Buddha's message, so old but yet so original, delivered in the simple spoken dialect of the people went deep down into their hearts.

There are historians who depict the Buddha as the founder of a new religion. But the Buddha never considered himself as such. He was in his opinion only reiterating the ancient noble-truths, *ārya satyas*. In the words of Rhys Davids, an acknowledged authority on the subject "Gautama was born and brought up and lived and died as a Hindu."

As has been already stated, metaphysical web-spinning was the favourite past-time of the intellectuals during the Buddha's day. The Buddha saw how people were wasting away their precious time in building the castles of speculation in thin air. He knew, as did the seers of the Upaniṣads, that the Infinite, whatever it might be called, lies somewhere in the beyond and that too it intellect cannot profitably be applied: *na medhāya na bahunā śrutena.* Truth, he asserted, has to be found in life itself. It cannot be obtained through arguments about matters outside the scope of life and hence beyond the ken of human intellect. "Whereof one cannot speak," he said, "thereof one must be silent." Preoccupation with metaphysical subtleties was not the correct approach towards a comprehension of the real. We have to realize the real in life and not through an avoiding of it; and what is life as we see it everyday? Is it not full of suffering, misery and pain? The eternal longing of human nature and the permanent postponement of the attainment of its wants, the vagaries of chance and the evanescence of things mundane and the oppressive weight of the monotonous daily round of duties, all these point towards the misery of existence. Situated as we are amidst this chaotic and miserable world, with no end in view and no guide to help us, what is the use of speculating over God and nature? Unable as we are to solve the tangles of the present sorrow and despair, is it not ridiculous for us to try to solve the mystery of existence? "It is not the time to discuss about fire for those who are actually in burning fire, but it is the time to escape from it," so says the *Majjhima Nikāya* (a Buddhist scripture). But the Buddha does not say that we have to stifle all our hopes and live on earth in weariness. No doubt life is an unending torrent of torments. But there is a way to extricate ourselves from this seemingly purposeless existence. Purpose, harmony and hope of beatitude can be instilled into this dry and prosaic life of ours. Of course, if we always brood over the emptiness of life and its accompanying misery one's mind will be at its tether. But we have to remember that, that which exists must have a cause. Suffering and pain are rampant in this world, no doubt. But why are they there? There must be a cause and a reason for their existence. They cannot be just unwarranted, having no justification for their existence. The world is "rolling from creation to decay" like the "sparkling and bursting bubbles" on a river. Nature is a continuous flow of events, a ceaseless rushing past of momentary states. But nature, though it is a flow, a stream and a vibration, is not without continuity. It is an indivisible whole. It is "a mighty maze but not without a plan." The world in spite of its fleeting nature is a cosmos. It has a law at the centre of it, animating it and dynamiting it. This law is the inexorable *niyama* that governs all phenomena and process. It is the rigorous and ruthless principle of *karma* that is working out for justice and balance in the world of human relations. This supreme principle, which is nothing but the *ṛta* of the *Ṛgveda,* is governing the whole universe. As soon as a *niyama* in the seemingly chaotic and aimless world is recognized, it brings lustre to our life. No more is our birth just an accidental resultant of the fusion of chance chromosomes. We did not begin with our birth. We were in the making for countless ages. Our birth and environment depended upon our past births and actions. The present is a child of the past, but we should not forget that it is the parent of the future. Our present is in accordance with the past and no doubt the yet undetermined and malleable future depends on the moulding which our present gives to it. It is on us that the responsibility to make our future rosier and happier devolves.

We have come into the world of our own irrational making. But who asked us to be content with it? Cannot we give a twist to it and construct a utopia, the *saṅgha*, out of it? And if we do not do so, resting content with our imperfect, surely it is we that are to be blamed. But how to do this? How to build up the *saṅgha*, the flawless perfect society? The Buddha says that it cannot be built up by fasting and penance, by preaching and worship. Neither can it be built by licentious self-indulgence. It is the middle path, the golden mean, between these two that has to be resorted to. Right belief and right aspiration, right conduct and right efforts constitute the way towards achieving the ideal *saṅgha*. Thus we see that the Buddha's teaching was nothing but the popularization of the Upaniṣadic ideal of spiritual democracy. "Go unto all lands," said the Buddha, "and preach this gospel. Tell them that the poor and the lowly, the rich and the high are all one." The Buddha's message was one of universal benevolence and love. His message has a profound significance to this atomic age of ours torn with strife and conflict. "Never in this world does hatred cease by hatred; hatred ceases by love," he declared, "let a man overcome anger by kindness, evil by good."

Not only did the Buddha strike at priesthood and gods, but his teaching condemned all private wealth, personal advantages and the hierarchical gradations of society. All men should belong to the one *saṅgha*, they should live together and lead a common life of righteousness. Live and while living love, this in essence is the Buddha's teaching. Thus it was not merely a moral but also a social revolution. Again, his *nirvāṇa* is not an esoteric communion with a fancied being called God, not is it the going into a hedonistic other-world. *Nirvāṇa* is the destruction of lust, hatred and ignorance. It is something to be achieved here and now in life. It is *mukti*, freedom from prejudice, ignorance, hatred and bad conduct; and this is to be obtained in this world alone. Otherwise how do we explain the fact that the Buddha attained perfection, *bodhi*, at thirty-five and lived for forty-five years more? *Nirvāṇa* is the highest kind of activity and to think that it can only synchronize with death is erroneous. Of course, the Buddha did not enlarge much on the conception of *nirvāṇa*, for he was sure that men could know it for themselves if they followed the right path he preached.

To the conservative people with vested interests, this doctrine of equality and love and the establishment of a new social order sounded their death-knell. The Buddha was dragging out all the egoistic reservations which they had made. To them he appeared as a terrible "moral huntsman driving out mankind out of the snow burrows in which they were sleeping hitherto." In this new ideal society of his, "there was to be no property, no privilege, no pride and precedence; no motive indeed and no reward but love." Priests realized that a greater spread of his doctrines meant the total annihilation of the priest-craft. The higher castes, similarly, realized that wider popularity of his teaching would mean the liquidation of the social barriers; and is it any wonder that in view of all this, he was made out to be the founder of a new and alien religion? In addition to this if we remember the fact that the Buddha hails from a ruling princely family, probably we can discern in his teaching a plain political bent. Connecting all these together, the temptation to see the anticipations of Communistic society in the *saṅgha* of the Buddha cannot be resisted. Probably the Buddha was the forerunner of not only Gandhi but also Marx, and is it too much to say that his doctrine represents a desirable synthesis of Gandhian idealism and Marxian materialism?

It is often said that the Buddha's doctrine is that of despair and life-negation. The Buddha denied the ethical value of austere asceticism. He never wanted people to become recluses. The very name, *vihāra* by which Buddhist monasteries were called shows that they were not intended to nourish sickly nuns and monks, who were a burden to society; and then the amazing buoyancy of spirit and vitality of life displayed by Japan, China and Burma, which have embraced Buddhism abundantly go to prove the dynamism of the Buddha's teachings. It might interest many to know that Genghis Khan, one of the greatest conquerors, was an adherent of Shamanism. Shamanism is a variety of Buddhism, found in Arctic Siberia, Mongolia and Soviet Central Asia, just like another variety of Buddhism, Lamaism, found in Tibet.

The extensive description on Buddhism shows that the Buddha never founded a new religion. The cardinal tenets preached by the Buddha are the same that have been preached by the Upaniṣads; and Buddhism merely represents a revival of the Upaniṣadic spiritualism and as such constitutes a new development or a restatement of Hinduism, suitable for that age. Our ancients who deemed the Buddha to be an *avatāra* of the Supreme, were no fools. Buddhism, therefore, is not at all an alien and a new rival religion, neither is it a differing creed. It forms one of the most vital phases in the evolution of Hinduism and is an advancement over the teaching of the Upaniṣads. In fact, it is the consummation of the Upaniṣads and as such an integral part of Hinduism. Writes Pandit Nehru in *The Discovery of India*:

> The conception of the Buddha, to which innumerable loving hands have given shape in carven stone and marble and bronze, seems to symbolize the whole spirit of Indian thought. Seated on the lotus flower, calm and impassive,

> above passion and desire, beyond the storm and strife of this world so far away he seems, out of reach, unattainable, yet again we look and behind those still, unmoving features there is a passion and an emotion, strange and more powerful than the passions and emotions we have known. His eyes are closed, but some power of the spirit looks out of them and a vital energy fills the frame.

Continues Nehru:

> The ages roll by, and the Buddha seems not so far away after all, his voice whispers in our ears and tells us not to run away from the struggle but, calm-eyed, to face it, and to see in life ever greater opportunities for growth and advancement.

4

Message of the Gītā

Just when this reorientation of outlook and the resuscitation of the ancient truth, *ārya satya*, were being formulated in the shape of Buddhism in the east, the same need of the age was being met by the composition of that immortal poem, the *Bhagavad-Gītā* in the west of India.

The *Bhagavad-Gītā* and Buddhism are the movements of the same spiritual re-emphasis and revival which took place as a reaction against ritualistic religion. Both of them adopt the middle path, the path of harmony between extreme self-denial and unbridled self-indulgence. The *Bhagavad-Gītā* just like the Buddha denounces fasting and other forms of torture which are mistakenly supposed to be *tapasyā*. Both the *Bhagavad-Gītā* and the Buddha laugh at the idea of supremacy by birth; and both care very little for the authority of the Vedas.

The only difference between the Buddha's approach and the approach of the *Bhagavad-Gītā* is that whereas the Buddha asks us not to think of transcendental reality and spoil our brain, the *Bhagavad-Gītā* asserts the existence of such a reality. No doubt it recognizes the three ways for the attainment of perfection, the path of intellect, the path of action and the path of faith. But its emphasis is specially on faith, *śraddhā* and *bhakti*.

Ruthless logic and dry dialectic demonstrate the exclusive existence of a featureless and formless reality — the Absolute. But why should this empty void, *nirguṇa Brahman*, devoid of all characteristics be taken as the supreme reality? If reason points towards a static and immobile reality, sense and empirical knowledge point towards a mobile and dynamic conception of reality. If reality is the impersonal and formless Absolute, what then is this world? Is it all a dream and a phantom? Is reality so limited that it exists only somewhere beyond this world? The *Bhagavad-Gītā* says that reality is as much dynamic as it is static. The world is no hallucination. Those who say that the world is a non-existent phantasm are according to the *Bhagavad-Gītā* ignorant. The world, with all its change and fleeting nature, is real in its entirety. The real is not exhausted in this world. The world is a manifestation and aspect of the supreme. But at the same time, the supreme stands towering beyond this empirical world, formless, unsullied and unmoving. The supreme, if it is to be adequately comprehended, should be understood as having two aspects: the manifested and the unmanifested. One side of the Divine is lost in creation, in the waves of becoming, of change; and the other side of it stands by itself immutable and eternal. The supreme is the synthesis of both. It is Puruṣottama, transcending the immutable (*akṣara*) and the mutable (*kṣara*). Vāsudeva, says Śaṅkarānanda in his commentary on *Bhagavad-Gītā*, "has two forms, the manifested and the unmanifested. The *para-Brahman* is the unmanifested and the whole world of moving and unmoving things (*cara* and *acara*) is the manifested." What the *Bhagavad-Gītā* wants to emphasize is that the Absolute is not some very remote and rare thing existing only in the blues, beyond the ken of human approach. It is here and before us as the world of things, which we daily experience. But it does not mean that it has exhausted itself herein. It stretches far beyond this world. It is Vāmana and also Trivikrama; and so if we want to understand the ultimate we have to grasp it not only as the formless immoveable being (*sat*) but we have to view it also as the fleeting world of change and movement, becoming or *asat*. As to how the Absolute can at the same time be the non-active immobile spirit and also the creative energy sustaining the universe is something which cannot be understood intellectually. It can be understood only through intuition. And if we have to say anything, we can only say that it is all *māyā*, that is to say, unexplainable; and there ends the matter.

If the cold and logical reason of man ends in the conception of an eternal substance subtly pervading the whole universe, the emotional demands of man require an object, personal and glowing on which they can vent themselves. Our emotional possibilities need not be stifled. They should also be provided with an adequate outlet. The Absolute, the *Brahman*, cannot be an object of this emotional outburst. No doubt a select few can meditate on the Absolute and satisfy themselves therewith. But the multitude require a concrete personality full of bliss and beauty and power. We can offer our devotion only to a personal God. There is no meaning in constructing altars to the unknown God as did the Greeks of old. Such a God cannot instil in us courage and hope. Man in the periods of his despondency, when his whole life seems to be purposeless, requires a guide and an anchor to steer him clear. Voltaire was not joking when he said, *si dieu n existait pas, il faudrait I inventer*. If God did not exist it would be necessary to invent him. That is why man's mind is always after some such mental image or conception which can satisfy him; and with mind's growth, this conception also widens till it embraces everything. Whether consciously or unconsciously most men worship something or other — some ideal whether it be national or international, this worldly or other-worldly. Is there any harm in substituting God for some such ideal? If we are worshipping God, it means we are worshipping the ideal concretization of goodness and beauty, truth and reality; and this is the God of the *Gītā*. He is the highest being, the illuminator of all souls and the life-giver for the entire world. He is pure love and sheer goodness. He is not the personification of the forces or objects of nature, as in the primitive Pagan religions. He is not the God who demanded human sacrifices from Abraham and Saul. He is not the Śiva who revelled in the man-sacrifices of Jarāsandha, neither is he the Kālī who revels in animal blood. He is the God, the father in heaven of Christ. He is the God, the tender boy cowherd of Mīrā Baī. He is Viṣṇu who runs to the succour of the little helpless Dhruva and Śiva who hearkens to the prayers of Nandanār. He is there to console everyone and comfort all. We have only to resort to Him, take refuge in Him and cry out for His help; and He is there with his ever-extended hand of mercy. At the same time He is not something quite foreign to us. He is there embedded in the caverns of our hearts. He throbs in our pulse and runs in our blood. But can He, the all-merciful, confine Himself exclusively to our domain? He is there in the dog and the dog-eater, in the learned brāhmin and the ruling prince; and not only in these but in all the animated and the unanimated — in the blossoming of the lotus, in the roaring of the sea and in the thundering of the sky. Conscious of His living presence everywhere, we have to surrender ourselves to Him. Unqualified surrender is what He demands. "Abandoning all *dharma*s seek me as thy sole refuge; I will liberate thee from all sins, do thou not grieve."[1] If we thus in all humility and faith sacrifice ourselves at His feet, we shall be lifted up and

1. *Bhagavad-Gītā*, 18:66.

be embraced by Him. When we thus fall at His feet, we fall to be propped up by the Infinite and suffused by the Divine.

This in short is the message of *Gītā*. But we have also to remember that it is a poem of crisis, not only of spiritual but also, of political and social crisis. It solves the practical day-to-day problems in the context of the spiritual background of human existence. It does not ask us to keep away from life. It is a clarion call to action — to meet the duties and obligations of life in accordance with the ideals of the age, keeping in view the spiritual background; and the action must be in a spirit of detachment, regardless of results. We have to surrender our totality to the Divine and function as mere instruments of it. How this is to be achieved, has been outlined elsewhere in this book.

Another interesting point about *Bhagavad-Gītā* is that it is not sectarian, though it is theistic. It is universal in its approach. So long as it is the true and living God, it does not care under which form we worship Him. It is indifferent whether we worship Him as Śiva with the trident or as Kṛṣṇa with the flute or as Allāh, the all-merciful. "All paths lead to Me," it says. Similarly its doctrines are not meant exclusively for any one community or caste. Its appeal is to man and woman, brāhmin and dog-eater, Indian and European alike. It is on account of this liberality of outlook and depth of vision, that it has found favour with all sects and retains its freshness even to this day. About the *Bhagavad-Gītā*, Pandit Nehru remarks:

> During the two thousand five hundred years since it was written. . . . Indian humanity went repeatedly through the processes of change and development and decay; experience succeeded experience, thought followed thought, but it always found something living in the *Gītā*, something that fitted into the developing thought and had a freshness and applicability to the spiritual problems that afflict the mind.

5

The Greek Connection

Some three hundred years after the Buddha, the Greeks came into contact with India and from then onwards for years Greece and India were in intimate touch. No doubt in the spheres of art and external living they influenced each other to a certain extent. But this did not go deep. Both the Indian and Greek cultures were sufficiently strong and highly developed to hold their own against each other and develop on their own distinctive lines. But still India contributed to a considerable extent to the Greek thought.

The outstandingly permanent feature which Greece gave to India is idol-worship. The Vedas, the Upaniṣads and early Buddhism were opposed to image and idol-worship. But the Greeks were consummate artists. Indeed the chief trait of Greek civilization is the predominance of artistic sense in every sphere. Their religion, their literature, in fact, their very life was artistic. I do not mean that the ancient Hindus were devoid of a sense of beauty. In fact, they were votaries of beauty. But this awareness of beauty, which they possessed, did not take any concrete shape. In Greece it was otherwise. Their sense of art overflowed. Its results were manifested in the high degree of perfection to which sculpture and architecture attained in their hands; and this artistic influence of Hellenic culture gradually had its way into India, through the Greek states like Afghanistan (Gandhāra) that were prospering on the Indian frontiers. Even then at first only Apollo-like statues of *bodhisattvas* were being made. But then the temptation to carve the Buddha himself in stone and bronze could not be resisted. The creative urge of the artists at last won the day and there appeared the statues and images of the Buddha. In view of all this it would not be mere speculation to suggest that image-worship came to India from Greece, according to some researchers.

In fact, there is nothing very much to be criticized in idol-worship. Just as God himself is not the reality but only a symbol to help towards conceiving reality, even so the idol or image, however beautiful it might be, is only a symbol to help towards conceiving God. Hinduism is aware of this truth. Just as Viṣṇu is a conception of the highest reality, *Brahman;* the *śāligrāma* is the symbol of that Viṣṇu. (Śaṅkara explains the relation between God and the reality, and the relation between God and the idol in the same words.) Every Hindu who worships in the temples knows fully well, that the stone image before him is not God Himself, but only a symbol of Him. That is why, the cone-shaped stones, which are worshipped as Śiva, are called *Śivaliṅgas. Śivaliṅga* means the symbol or representation of Śiva. Indeed if the idols could impress upon the naïve and simple mind of man the awe of the Infinite and the mystery of the Divine, and if they could establish in men's minds the conception of God — that is enough justification for the existence and worship of the idols. Nobody who has entered the massive rock temples of south India and has felt the overwhelming abundance of form and splendour can decry the utility of temples. Just like Hinduism, the Hindu temple is based on the principle of unity in diversity. The soul who has felt the rapturous ecstasy of the identity of the self with the

Divine and has thereby attained the vision of inner unity, will view the manifoldness of objects as the manifestation of the one fundamental unity. It is this awareness that is objectified in the temple architecture. The exterior of the temple exuberates with form. Each pillar is chiselled out of solid rock and is decorated with a thousand forms. In Madurai and Kāñcīpuram there are about thousand pillars in each temple. Each pillar overflows with inexhaustible opulence of detail and ornament. No two pillars resemble each other. There is a staggering variety of theme; and as soon as one enters, one is overwhelmed by the gigantic massiveness of this mass of carven rock. A sense of infinity, mystery and awe is inevitably forced on us. Quite unawares, we feel an inclination to bend and bow down in utter humility to the master of all this dominating pile of rock, form and variety. But when we enter into the inner precincts, the shrine within, the *sanctum sanctorum*, we see that it is nothing but a small dark cell. No outside air or light is allowed within; and when we return back, we again encounter the ornament and splendour that surrounds the temple. But it is no longer the bewildering variety of decoration and detail. It now serves to manifest the real which is the transcendental totality of all forms.

This is the purpose that is served by the temples. Like the shady silences of the forest, the lofty rugged heights of the mountains and the unpeeled wave-beaten sandy shores of the ocean, the temples also provide us the healing balm for the numberless wounds caused by contacts with a harsh and unkind world. The temples suffuse us with a serene peace and enshroud us with an infinite sweetness. It was for this purpose that they were designed and constructed; and so long as they fulfil this task of theirs, crowds will flock to them and be comforted.

6

The Great Epics

THE *Rāmāyaṇa* and the *Mahābhārata* — the two great epics of India relate incidents which took place centuries before Christ. But combined with these central events are recorded many incidents that took place during great stretches of time. Anyway they are a vast and miscellaneous collection of ancient lore. Probably they took shape somewhere in the fifth and sixth centuries BC. Whoever might be the authors or whenever they might have been written, they are the books which exercise a living influence on every Indian. Few read them in the original Sanskrit. But in their many translations they exercise a pervasive force in all the Indian villages and form part of the texture of the rustic's life. It is with the stories in them that our children are regaled, and it is again with their anecdotes that our aged are comforted. Not all the stories they relate are true. Facts and fiction are interwoven in them. Most of the stories are heroic in conception and teach adherence to truth and the pledged word and inculcate principles of courage, goodness and sacrifice for the common end. It was the stories of Abhimanyu, Arjuna and Rāma that produced a Rāṇā Pratāp and a Śivājī. It was the legends of Sītā, Sāvitrī and Damayantī that gave us a Rānī Padminī of Chittor and a Rānī Lakṣmī Bāī of Jhānsī; and the stories and books that can produce such magnificent types of personality, must surely have deep reserves of inner strength and wisdom.

The *Rāmāyaṇa* and the *Mahābhārata* are the luxurious growths of an abundant life and rich imagination. They not only tell us of the minds and hearts and purposes of our fore-fathers and provide us with a basis for thought and action; but they also are the dreams, allegories and symbols of a something beyond, which Vālmikī and Vyāsa saw, with their vivid poetic insight. The gods and goddesses, the heroes and heroines of the *Rāmāyaṇa* and the *Mahābhārata* are the concretizations of Vālmikī's dreams and Vyāsa's imaginations of Indian ethos. The traditional story connected with the origin of *Rāmāyaṇa* gives us a clue to this:

One beautiful sunny morning the sage Vālmikī accompanied by his disciples comes to the flowing stream adjacent to his forest home, for the morning bath. The rays of the early sun are dancing on the fresh dewy leaves of spring. The deers are grazing nearby. The *kokil*s are cooing. The fresh pure waters of the stream are running past, glittering in the sunlight. A happy pair of *krauñca* birds are wooing in a yonder tree. The whole jungle is full of harmony, peace and balance; but, there suddenly arrives on the scene a niṣāda with his cruel bow and arrow, and taking a sure aim and a steady look at the happy pair of birds he drops the male bird dead with his bloody arrow. The female bird breaks out into heart-piercing cries and rends the poetic heart of Vālmikī in twain. No doubt, it is a simple incident. But it stirs Vālmikī to depths, and he bursts out with a curse, which later took the form of a song, full of incomparable beauty, pathos and majesty; and the result is the *Rāmāyaṇa*, sublime as the Himalayas and vast as the Indian ocean.

The *Mahābhārata* has a particular significance. In it Vyāsa has tried to weave together many prevailing Aryan and Draviḍian systems of belief and forms of worship into one single fabric — Hinduism. It also tries to emphasize the cultural unity of India — *Bhārata Deśa.*

There is a tendency among our modern young men to disparage and look down upon these ancient epics of ours. But it is these two books that have catered to the needs of the learned brāhmin and the uneducated alike and have built up a unity of outlook and a tenacity of purpose among our people, which alone led them to survive and overshadow all the adverse diversity through which India passed. They have pulled our fathers many a time from the drudgery and ugliness of everyday existence and have showed them the path of endeavour and right living. Books which are entirely false and spurious, cannot be so fruitful and inspiring. Using Goethe's words uttered in a similar connection, if Vālmikī and Vyāsa "were great enough to invent things like that, we at least should be great enough to believe them."

7

Mahāyāna: The Integral Whole

In 184 BC the empire of Mauryans ended. By that time disruptive tendencies in the gospel of the Buddha set in. The indifference of the Buddha to metaphysical problems and his silence over supra-mental truths were interpreted in a negative way. Scepticism and agnosticism were attributed to the Buddha. Pure-phenomenalism was made out to be the creed of the Buddha. No doubt the Buddha said that the whole world is a process, a stream of events. But he also posited that there was a law governing the process. His emphasis on *dharma* and *niyama* was overlooked. The whole world was made out to be a great ship-wreck. The only important thing considered was to be the saving of oneself from this chaotic world. Monastic tendencies were over-powered. A morbid suppression of all interest in life and an indifference to all world's affairs, was held out to be the ideal. Thus the whole teaching of the Buddha, wherein he preached a harmonious middle-path was interpreted in a way which was entirely antagonistic to it. No wonder this original and debased form of Buddhism was called the Hīnayāna.

The imperial patronage of the great Aśoka made the tenets of the Buddha the common religion of the common man. But the gloomy negativistic and narrowly pessimistic interpretation of the Buddha's doctrine made the people indifferent to life.

Each one was encouraged to seek his individual salvation and let the world go on. All these tendencies sapped the vitality of the people. This explains how the Indo-Bactrians, the Indo-Parthians and the Kuṣāṇas were able to overrun the country and establish their principalities. But then there emerged from the Kuṣāṇa dynasty, a great prince who was able to establish his sway almost throughout the north. This was Kaniṣka who had his capital at Peshawar.

All these foreign peoples who came to India as invaders in the end settled down in India and embraced the Hindu culture and religion. Much of the strength pertinacity and liberality of out look in Hinduism owes its existence to the absorption of these strong and sturdy foreign peoples — the Greeks, the Parthians and the Śakas — into the Hindu fold.

Kaniṣka was a typical Hindu. He not only used to worship the Buddha, but was also offering incense to the old Vedic gods. On some of his coins he is depicted in the act of standing before the fire and offering incense. In his reign Buddhism was purged of its negativistic tendencies and pessimistic outlook and captured again the spirit of the Buddha's teaching.

This was chiefly due to Nāgārjuna. He was mainly responsible for making Buddhism the broad-way or the Great-way, the Mahāyāna, for all peoples. Under his inspiring guidance Buddhism spread out in every direction. It became tolerant and adaptable to the needs of the country. The original spirit of the Buddha was again re-instilled into his followers.

Nāgārjuna was an Āndhra and was the president of the famous Amarāvati University. Nāgārjuna and Śaṅkara are by far the greatest philosophers that India has ever produced. The well-known Russian professor Stcherbatsky says that Nāgārjuna's place is "among the great philosophers of humanity."

The Mahāyāna lays its stress on the existence of a supramental reality. Aśvaghoṣa calls it *tathatā* or Suchness and Nāgārjuna calls it *śūnyatā* or Void. The nature of this transcendental reality is beyond language and description. None of the categories of space and time can be applied to it. It is devoid of all the limitations and contingencies of empirical experience. As such it is called the great void or *mahāśūnya*. But it does not mean that it is pure nothingness. It is something entirely beyond the phenomenal world, but comprises it. Since no other word can be found for it, we are forced to call it nothingness. But metaphysically it is something that is transcendent and immanent in all things; and if anybody wants to describe it, he can only say that it is like itself; *tathatā* or suchness.

But all this cannot satisfy the common man. He cannot soar in the rarefied heights of thought and perceive the *mahāśūnya*, behind the mists and fogs of mental categories and symbols. Man wants something concrete to which he could offer incense and flowers. So the Buddha is considered as the realization of the ideal, he is deemed to be the personification of the law (the *niyama*, the *dharma*) inherent throughout the cosmos. The Buddha is made out to be the God and devotion to him is encouraged. About the same time images of the Buddha began to appear from the Grecian north-west. They were installed in public places and openly worshipped. Thus the Buddha is conceived as the supreme one. He is the creator and sustainer of the whole universe. He is immanent in all beings. But since he is also the highest reality, he is much more than the whole universe; and the way to bliss is to believe in him and take refuge in him. The *Lalitavistara* records the saying of the Buddha thus: "To all who believe in *Me I* do good, while friends ere they to *Me* who seek refuge in *Me*." But at the same time, we should not eschew our social life.

We should take active part in the world evolving new social and religious ideals; and even if we feel that there is nothing to be gained personally, we should not give up our social duties and retire into the shell of our egoism. We should work not only for ourselves but for the whole humanity; for are not all men our kindred and does not the same the Buddha, the *devātīdeva,* live and throb in the hearts of all?

Thus in the end, the Buddha became another name for Reality, just as Śiva or Viṣṇu. He was made out to be another form of Viṣṇu just like Kṛṣṇa or Rāma. He was not at all considered to be different from Viṣṇu or Śiva. That is why there was not much protest when the famous Buddha temple at Purī was converted into a Kṛṣṇa temple, nor was there any crusade when the Buddhist *stūpa* of Amarāvatī was worshipped as a *Śivaliṅga*. "Truth is one; (though) the wise call it by various names, Agni, Yama, Indra and Vāyu," says the *Ṛgveda*; and this teaching was not lost on our fore-fathers. In fact, there is no difference between the teaching of the Upaniṣads and the teaching of the Buddha and there is no difference between their religious aspects too, i.e. the Mahāyāna and the *Bhagavad-Gītā*.[1]

If from about 150 CE to 484, North India enjoyed peace and prosperity under the Kuṣāṇas and the Guptas, and if at about the same period south India also enjoyed happiness and plenty under the Sātavāhanas, Pāṇḍyans, Coḷas and Cheras — it was because the truths of the Upaniṣads were still remembered and the people followed indiscriminately the Śaiva, the Vaiṣṇava or the Buddhist cults as they pleased, keeping in mind the fact that all these creeds were but parts of that integral whole — the Hinduism.

1. Radhakrishnan, *Indian Philosophy*, vol. I; "The Conception of Buddhist *Nirvāṇa* and *Sādhanā*" in *Viśva-bhāratī Quarterly*, 1924.

8

Advent of Islam: Śaṅkara

FROM the first century CE, waves after waves of adventurous Indians went towards the East and South-East Asia and colonized Ceylon, Burma, Malaya, Java, Sumatra, Borneo, Siam, Cambodia and Indo-China. Trade and commerce were the supreme passion of Indians in those days. It was commercial enterprise and quest for new commodities (like millets, fine cotton, gold etc.) that made the Indians of those days to undertake these extraordinary expeditions across the perilous seas. On important trade routes, widely scattered colonies were started simultaneously. Old Indian names were given to these settlements. Though it was mainly for trade and adventure that Indians went to these eastern lands, sometimes the desire to continue their culture was also responsible for their sojourns to these foreign countries. In the sixth century CE there were more than 3,000 Buddhist monks and 10,000 Indian families in the Lo Yang province of China. The early colonists settled down and greater numbers came in their wake. The Indians imported their own culture and art into these colonies. Some of these colonies adopted the Vedic creed of Indra and Varuṇa. Some other colonies adopted the Buddhist creed of Mahāyāna. The two existed side by side as friends for years, and a hybrid form of worship grew up. The Indians freely mixed with the people there and a new mixed culture was the resultant.

From the Greek and Arab accounts we know that regular maritime relations existed between India, the far-east and the further countries. The Arab culture, like any other culture, say the Phoenician, the Chaldean or the Hebrew, had a long past. As is often erroneously supposed, the Arabs were not barbaric and uncivilized people before Muhammad. They were highly advanced people even in pre-Islamic days. Arabic was a highly developed language and the Arabs were very great travellers. Like the Phoenicians they went far across the seas in search of trade. There was an Arab colony in South China, near Canton, in pre-Islamic days.

Then suddenly Muhammad appeared in Arabia and vitalized his people and filled them with a new faith and energy. The revolutionary character of Muhammad and his message of human brotherhood dynamited the Arabs. Unable to contain within themselves the new momentum imparted to them, the Arabs in a frenzy of enthusiasm spread out and conquered all the lands from Spain to Mongolia and preached their message of human brotherhood. Years before Muhammad Bin Kasim invaded Sindh, these Arab traders came into contact with Kerala. There were no military conquests. But still, the influence of this cultural contact went so far that the last of the Cheraman Perumal kings of Malabar was a convert to Islam and died on a voyage to Mecca. The title of Zamorin of Calicut bears witness to this influence. Even to this day, the Zamorins are anointed kings by a Moplah. Kāladi, a small town, then formed part of a principality, whose king was also a convert to Islam. All these facts show the extent to which Islam influenced south India then.

It was in this time that Śaṅkara was born at Kāladi. In the sixth and seventh centuries Hinduism was in a chaotic state. In the south there was a decline of Buddhism. Śaiva and

Vaiṣṇava cults were the order of the day. Devotion to God was supposed to be the path to salvation. Truth was being veiled in mists of sentiment and fogs of superstition. Interested priests were spreading their tentacles everywhere through festivals and temples. Bodies were being branded with hot metallic designs to make one a Vaiṣṇava or a Śaiva. In the Deccan, Śiva was being worshipped in a very unclean manner as a dog. Kāpālikas were offering human victims to their God Bhairava. A perverted group of Śāktas were carrying on detestable practices in the name of the Goddess. As a reaction to all this Mīmāṁsakas like Kumārila and Maṇḍana were advocating a go-back campaign towards the Vedic sacrifices. The rigid social barriers erected by caste grew ruthlessly and stifled the life of the Hindu society.

At the same time the impact of Islam on India through the Arab traders was profound. It was impossible for acute and sensible minds not to be influenced by the new culture and religion of the indefatigable Arabs.

Śaṅkara was the first who awoke to the national unity of India and the religious unity of Hinduism. He saw around him diverse currents of thought troubling India and disintegrating its harmony. His mission was to synthesize these diverse currents and build-up a unity of outlook out of that diversity. He saw the Vaiṣṇavas, the Śaivas and the Śāktas. He knew that the same God was being worshipped by all of them under different names. He was aware that truth can wear vestures of many colours and speak in strange tongues. But he was pained to see the wrangling between the Vaiṣṇavas and Śaivas, about the supremacy of Viṣṇu and Śiva. There were sometimes furious quarrels between the rival paṇḍits. He preached that all these gods were but the representations of the one Real. He composed hymns of infinite beauty and grandeur in praise of all these deities and encouraged the worship of all these gods. He made the orthodox Vedic paṇḍits also accept these deities; and today even the most orthodox brāhmin does not worship the Indra or Varuṇa daily. He offers his daily worship to Viṣṇu or Kālī, Śiva or Sūrya. Śaṅkara was a man of amazing activity and inexhaustible energy. He incessantly travelled over the whole of India. He met countless people, argued, debated, reasoned, convinced and filled them with a portion of his tremendous vitality and zeal. He was intensely conscious of his mission. He looked upon the whole of India from Cape Comorin to the Himalayas as a single unit. He knew that there was a common spirit pervading this whole subcontinent. He wanted to stamp on this vast tract of land a common outlook and suffuse it with a common religion. He tried and remarkably succeeded in making India a well-knit whole. He worked alike in the intellectual, philosophical and religious fields and brought about a greater unity of thought everywhere.

If it was the Buddha who raised his protest against sacrifices, it was Śaṅkara who contributed towards their disappearance with his emphasis on the uselessness of ritual for liberation. When travel was difficult and means of transport primitive what was that force which made Śaṅkara to undertake adventurous journeys through hills and forests and alien kingdoms and made him preach with fervour and faith his forceful but ancient truth? This revolutionary urgency and insurmountable zeal which Śaṅkara displays are due to the influence of Islam. No preacher before Śaṅkara, not even the Buddha, was seized with the vital urge to propagate his doctrines all over India. Śaṅkara was the first Hindu who travelled debating, convincing and converting people to his *jñāna-mārga* all over India — from Śṛṅgerī to Badrināth and from Dwārakā to Purī. "Is it fanciful," asks Prof. Humayun Kabir, "to find in Śaṅkara's fervour and zeal traces of the influence of the revolutionary zeal of Islam"? Then again what was it that enabled Śaṅkara to escape from the nauseating diversity of the various warring creeds, and made him rediscover the ancient Vedic injunction, the Real is one, and wise call it by many names? Can it be Islam which reminded him that Vedic truth? Śaṅkara was a great logician and dialectician. But he always bent himself before the scriptures. He knew that intellect was inadequate to comprehend the Real and that intuition was necessary. He continually harps upon the authoritativeness of revealed scripture, *Śabda Pramāṇa* — and bases all his philosophic constructions on the Śruti. Rāmānuja acknowledged the authority of other books besides the Veda, the Āgamas. Madhva accepts *Bhāgavata* as the personification of God (*Bhagavān*), Himself. But for Śaṅkara the scripture, Śruti is supreme to which he subordinates all other literature. His passion for the texts of the Vedānta reminds us of the Muslim's adoration of his one book — the *Qurān*. All these facts put together — his insistence on the unity of *Brahman*, his unqualified acceptance of the texts of Vedānta, his missionary zeal and the prevalence of Islam as a living force in his birth place — force us to think that he was very much influenced by Islam. Writes Prof. Humayun Kabir:

> Few suspect any external influence on the Vedānta of Śaṅkara and yet there are reasons to suppose that he was influenced by the impact of Islam on the prevalent modes of thought.

The advent of Islam in India was mainly responsible for bringing together the different heterogeneous sects worshipping different gods. Śaṅkara suffused into all these sects a sense of unity, and put a stop to their wrangling, worthless and endless debates. The various systems of worship — Śaiva, Vaiṣṇava, Sūrya and Śākta no more looked upon themselves as conflicting sects. If today the Iyengar and Iyer, the Sastri and Acharya, the Kaśmīrian Śaiva and Bengali Śākta — look upon themselves as the adherents of the same religion in spite of their antagonistic metaphysical beliefs and incompatible daily ritual, it is because of the genius of Śaṅkara. He was also the first man who awoke to the national unity of India, in spite of the various races that inhabit it. No doubt the *Mahābhārata* makes a definite attempt to emphasize the fundamental unity of India or Bhāratavarṣa. Previously the region to the north of the Vindhyas was considered to be a different country. The war of the Kurus or at any rate the writing of the *Mahābhārata* marks the beginning of the conception of India as a whole — the Bhāratavarṣa. The extension of the kingdom of Aśoka through Kaliṅga (Orissa) upto the Andhra and the unparalleled travels of Śaṅkara throughout the whole of India, the acceptance of his doctrines by the major part of the country and the establishment of four *maṭhas* or spiritual centres by him at the four corners of India (Badrināth, Purī, Dwārakā and Śṛṅgerī) established the conception of the cultural unity of India. Previous to that the people of Magadha used to think of the Kaliṅgas as the inhabitants of a different country (*paradeśa*). The people of Vaṅga thought that the people of Aṅga were aliens, and the Āndhras used to hate the Keralas as foreigners. But after Śaṅkara, everyone in India felt he was the resident of the same country. Śaṅkara did all this some twelve hundred years ago. But the impress of his powerful mind and rich personality on India is evident everywhere even today.

The diversity of India is tremendously obvious, but it lies at the surface only. There is a bewildering variety of dress, habits and language if we survey the people that are scattered between the Tamilian far south and the Paṭhān of north-west. But even to the most casual observer the presence of a unity that defies description is evident. Writes Frederick Whyte in *The Future of East and West*:

> The greatest of all contradictions in India is that over this diversity is spread a great unity, which is so great a reality, and so powerful.

Supreme though Śaṅkara is as a theologian, dialectician and mystic, his greatest achievement lies in the welding together of the heterogeneous sects into a unified mass (Hinduism) and in his propagation of the conception of a unified India — Bhārata-mātā. Unsurpassed though Śaṅkara's theology is for its mystic insight combined with its metaphysical depth and logical power, it is only a recreation of the forgotten body of knowledge found in the Upaniṣads.

9

Bhakti: Hindustānī Culture

AFTER the invasion of Sindh by the Arabs in CE 712, came the Turks under the leadership of Mahmud of Ghazni three hundred years later and then the Afghans at the end of the twelfth century. The Arab and Turki invasions did not have any effect on India. The Arabs reached only Sindh and occupied it and even that fell away from their empire within fifty years or so. The invasion of the Turks under the leadership of Ghazni resulted in the segregation of the Punjab for a while. But the Afghans who came later in CE 1191 were an Indo-Aryan race. They came from Afghanistan, which under the name of Gandhāra formed part of India in the ancient days. Their language Pushto was a derivative from Sanskrit. So their invasion was like a cousin fighting with another cousin; and as it often occurs when cousins fight, they were ruthless in their behaviour towards the conquered. But soon they cooled down. India became their home and Delhi their capital. Vincent Smith says:

> These foreigners like their fore-runners the Śakas and the Yueh-chi, universally yielded to the wonderful assimilative power of Hinduism, and rapidly became Hinduized.

This process of Hinduization was rapid. Alāuddīn Khiljī, one of their great rulers, married a Hindu lady and so did his son. Later rulers, no doubt, like Qutub-ud-Dīn, Sultāna Raẓiā and

Iltutmiś were Turks. But the nobles and officers of state and the army were Afghans.

It is wrong to call these Turki and Afghan invasions as the Muslim invasions. Neither can the British occupation of India be called a Christian invasion. The Turks and Afghans invaded India only to exploit her and establish kingdoms. But somehow the Afghan rulers merged themselves in India and began in course of time to look upon India as their home and the rest of the world as foreign. Feroz Shah and Ghayas-Uddīn, the Tughlak had Hindu mothers. In south India the Nawāb of Gulbarga married the Hindu princess of Vijayanagar. A gradual fusion between Islam and Hinduism began to take place under the auspices of the Afghan dynasties. By then both Islam and Hinduism were well-defined and well-formulated. So neither could be amalgamated into one. Both of them refused to be parts of a single religion. But still each influenced the other. Islam brought with it the dynamic message of social democracy. Like an explosive force it blew away the existing social bonds — which the Buddha tried to break earlier — into thin air. Large numbers of the oppressed and backward castes, unable to resist the temptation to enjoy equality of social status, joined its ranks. Most of these Muslim converts were bred and brought up in Hinduism. In spite of these mass conversions, the Indian Muslims remained dominantly Hindu in outlook and way of life, in spite of change in religion. Most of these simple rural folk probably thought that Allāh was another new name added to the existing list of thousand names, like Kṛṣṇa, Keśava, Viṣṇu and Govinda. The transcendental outlook of Hinduism powerfully influenced Islam and made it mystical; and as a result, Sufism emerged. The basis of Sufism is *Qurān*, no doubt, and neo-Platonism also contributed to its growth. But its whole attempt and ideal, i.e. the merging of the individual in the Absolute, is evidently Hindu. Just as the fierce monotheism of Islam affected Śaṅkara, the supra-theistic outlook of Hinduism influenced the Indian Muslims. As a consequence Islam in India became something different from Islam in other lands. Is it wrong to call this Islam the Indo-Islam?

Similarly the completely non-ascetic and forceful social aspect of Islam influenced Hinduism, to a great extent. The growth of Bengal Vaiṣṇavism, the development of the Maharashtra *bhakti* school and the formation of Kabīr-Pantha are all due to this.

The attempts of Kabīr, and Nānak who is alleged to be his disciple, are noteworthy. These two endeavoured to fuse Islam and Hinduism together and evolve a new religion. In a conscious and systematic way they tried to create a new religion out of the two. Nānak's attempts ended in an epic-phenomenon — the emergence of Sikhism. Years later Akbar tried again to do the same. But he was less successful than Kabīr. A religion can only emerge, or develop or grow. It cannot just be invented or created overnight. Habits can be created, customs can be formed and conventions can be set-up, but none can set-up a religion. That is why Kabīr's attempts met with partial success and Akbar's attempts were more fruitless, for he had neither the magnetic personality nor the mystic vision of Kabīr. It is curious to note that in our own days, Vivekānanda had the same hopes:

> For our own mother-land a junction of the two great systems, Hinduism and Islam — Vedānta brain and Islam body — is the only hope. I see in my mind's eye the future perfect India rising out of this chaos and strife, glorious and invincible, with Vedānta brain and Islam body.
>
> — "Letters of Swami Vivekānanda," Almora

The impact of Islam on Hinduism was responsible for another important development — the formulation of the theory of *līlā* in Vaiṣṇavism. In the Upaniṣadic idealism there is no adequate explanation for the phenomenal world. If Reality is *Brahman*, the eternal and immutable, what then is this world of changing events? Is it unreal just like the barren woman's son? The Upaniṣads and also Nāgārjuna and Śaṅkara say that this world of events is not unreal. They add that it is also not the real, because what is real should be permanent and unchanging. What then is this world, as we see it, if it is neither real nor unreal? The answer is that the world is a phenomenon which cannot be explained. It is *māyā* and *anirvacanīya.* They are also unable to explain as to why and how this unexplainable world arose, because how can an unexplainable thing be accounted for or explained? So the Upaniṣads and *Bhagavad-Gītā* say that the Real is not only transcendental, but is also pervasive throughout this world. Reality is not some static immobility stationed somewhere beyond this world. No doubt it stands unchanged and permanent beyond this world, but at the same time it has manifested itself as this world. In other words Reality has two aspects; the mobile and the immobile: the concrete and the abstract. It combines both and transcends them. It is analogous to the conception of the Mermaid. But the question arises as to how these incompatibles exist together? We are told that our intellect cannot function in that sphere; and that intuitive vision only can silence these doubts.

This difficulty arises even if we accept theism. If there is a God, what is the relation between him and this world? If he has created the world, why did he do so? Even the fool does not do anything without a purpose. As such there must be a purpose for which God created the world. If it be said that he created it for his own satisfaction, it means that he was in an unsatisfactory condition at one time. That is derogatory to his perfection. If on the other hand it is said that God created the world for our sake, he becomes an instrument to cater to our needs; and God cannot be subservient to anything. For the old question, "why God made the world,"? the answer is found in the *līlā* theory of the Vaiṣṇavas.

The world, according to this theory, is the pure play of the Divine, who is undetermined and indeterminate. The world is the pure unpurposive activity of the Divine and therefore constitutes the play or sport (*līlā*) of the Divine. The happy cowherd breaks out into a tune. There is no motive for his doing this. His exuberance of vitality just overflows in this way. The healthy little child kicks his hands and legs this way and that. There is no purpose in these movements. The fullness of life and health in the child are just finding an outlet in this way. The case is the same here. The Divine is joy and life. The sheer joy and abundance of life in the Divine are expressing themselves as the world. God is so full that his fullness is overflowing; and this overflowing fullness has expressed itself as the universe. The ocean is so deeply profound, that it cannot contain the profundity to itself. It has to resound continuously with the throbbing of this deep profundity of itself. Similarly, God is full of so many possibilities that he cannot but actualize Himself as the world. Potentiality cannot for ever remain so. One day it has to become kinetic. Its very nature forces it to become so. Even so the Spirit (or God) cannot contain within itself its fullness of joy and life. Purposelessly and spontaneously this abundance is expressing itself as the world. The world is the manifestation of the unpurposive activity of the Divine and as such constitutes its play. The *prapañca* is the *līlā* of *Bhagavān*.

This *līlā* theory cannot be traced to the Upaniṣads or the *Bhagavad-Gītā*. Suddenly this beautiful idea appears in the Vaiṣṇava literature. The extremely practical and worldly outlook of Islam forced the sensitive minds of the Vaiṣṇava poets to think about the relation of the Theos and Cosmos, God and the world. Their fertile brains and mystic tendency led them to the *līlā* theory.

Since the great majority of Indian Muslims were converts from Hinduism and since the other Muslims lived for a very long time together, the Hindus and Muslims developed many common traits, habits and ways of living. Music, architecture, dress and traditions were influenced by this common culture. They lived together peacefully, joined each other's festivals, did the same kind of work and spoke the same language. This was possible because the Afghan kings and later the Mongol kings (Mughals) considered India as their homeland and looked upon all Indians — Muslim and Hindu — as their subjects. The foresight and vision of Babar and Akbar did much towards the building up of a synthetic spirit and common culture; and this justifies our speaking of a continuous Indian culture or as Babar in his autobiography calls it the "Hindustānī Culture."

The prosaic short-sightedness and the orthodox bigotry of Aurangzeb and the Hindu nationalism of the Marāṭhās, which was a reaction against Aurangzeb's bigotry, contributed towards the disruption of this common culture. Since then British diplomacy has been trying to complete this task of disruption. But India is fortunate as this has not happened.

10

The British and Reformation

THE British success in the battle of Plassey in 1757 marked the beginnings of British rule in India. Before the British advent in India there was a temporary balance and synthesis in India. Under the Great Mughals the country reached political stability. The loosening of the social bonds and the not-infrequent marriages between the Muslims and Hindus, which were encouraged by the diplomacy of Akbar and others constructed an equilibrium in social life. The various religious cults of the saints and mystics — Bengal Vaiṣṇava, Karnataka Vīra Śaiva and Maharastra *bhakti* movements, the Dādu-Pantha, the Kabīra Pantha, etc. worked out for a rapprochement between Islam and Hinduism.

Then Aurangzeb came and tried to set the clock of progress back. As a reaction to this in the Marāṭhās started a revivalist tendency to fight back Islam. The letter of Śivājī written to Rājā Jaya Siṁha, Aurangzeb's *sūbedār* in Deccan makes this point clear. He writes:

> "Let us unite for the protection of the Hindus and the upholding of Hinduism." [*do dil yak besa kumkohra, paragadgī arad anvohara; ajin dar mara guftanika vasest, kī dar namhe-avurdanas rai nest.*] "If you have a sharp sword and if you have manliness in you, then show it by destroying Islam and Muslim." (*ci kardi basahejahan yad kun, agar baharedari je*

farjanagi; jani lafe mardi vo mardanagi, je soje vatanlegra tav deh).

Thus Aurangzeb's intolerance and isolationism mirrored themselves in Śivājī.

Then came the impact of the West on India. This was the last straw on the camel's back. The balance and synthesis, which were almost achieved and which were just then going to pieces under the influences of the narrow and bigoted outlooks of Aurangazeb and Śivājī were completely destroyed by this sudden appearance of Europe on the Indian scene. New forces and pent-up energies were released; and a fresh process of reaction and synthesis began, which has not yet stopped.

In the days of old, each fresh race of invaders only ended by becoming Indians, but also Hindus. Their ways and outlooks were incorporated into the Hindustānī culture (to use Bābar's words), and not only they became Hindus, but also Hinduism too was modified. First came the Draviḍians to India, they settled down, merged with the natives and developed a very high culture; the Indus Valley culture. Then the Aryans came, they too settled down, fused with the Draviḍians and gave rise to the Hindu culture and religion. Succeeding hordes of people afterwards like Indo-Scythians, Indo-Parthians and Kuṣāṇas also came down and ended by becoming Hindus and champions of Hinduism (Rājpūts). Then the Afghan and Turki and Turko-Mongol invaders came. But these people refused to become Hindus, they were the first people who resisted the assimilative power of Hinduism. But they could not help being Indianized. The stamp of India was duly impressed upon them and differentiated them from the outside Islamic world. They never became Hindus but as Vincent Smith puts it, "they rapidly became Hinduized."

But the case of Europeans who came to India was different. They never came with the intention of settling down here or setting up an Empire. If today there is the British Empire in India, it is a mere accident. The Europeans who came, came for exploitation. As such they looked down upon the Indians and remained aloof from them. By deliberate choice they remained alien and indifferent to Indian culture. Only economic and commercial relations prevailed between them and Indians. They neither wanted to Europeanize India, nor did they want to be Indianized. They looked upon India as a battlefield, where they can just win and carry the booty home. Thus for the first time in India two closed systems faced each other.

But this could not last for long. If India had been a free land, she would have at her will chosen the good in the West. But her political subjugation by the West made her accept what was imposed. Village autonomy, village industries and the joint family were given powerful jolts. This led to the breakdown of the joint life and corporate character of the village communities. Rural economy was destroyed and agriculture was made to suffer. In the place of village industries attempts to construct large scale capitalistic or state industries were not made.

The old pattern of social, political and economic life was disturbed and to an extent destroyed. No attempts to construct a new and integrated system of life and culture were evolved. A vacuum was therefore the result. But nature abhors a vacuum. We shall see how this is being filled up. All these facts are necessary to understand the changes which took place in the Hindu religion and culture. There are some who believe that religion has nothing to do with economics and politics. But this mistaken notion is held by very few sane men those days.

It was in this context that Macaulay and Bentinck introduced Western education in India. This led to momentous results. The first acquaintance with European thought dazzled many Indians. An uncritical adoration of the West and infantile enthusiasm for everything European was the result. The impatient ambition of the early number of English-educated class was to Westernize India and Christianize Hinduism. They were no doubt patriotic, but were denationalized in outlook. They accepted at least in practice what the Europeans told them; that the past culture of India was only a half-civilization. They strove to rid India of all that did not square with their Westernized outlook. They sought to simplify and bare Hinduism of all its complexities and depth of spirit. They created a literature which was nothing but an eager importation of all the ideas and forms of the English literature. They tried to incorporate the semi-democracy of nineteenth-century England into India. This mentality is reflected in the Brahmo Samāja. Rammohun Roy's idea in establishing it was to adapt Hinduism on rationalistic social reform basis to the new outlook. His successor Kesab Chandra Sen gave it a more Christian outlook. These tendencies brought in a spirit of free intellectual activity and subjected the established dogmas and conventions to rigorous criticism.

These reformist tendencies made people turn their eyes and survey the past; and the forgotten past stood like an enchanting dream before their eyes. The infantile admiration for everything European could not last long. Reaction is implicit in human nature itself. As a reaction to the influences of Christianity, an indiscriminate defence of everything ancient resulted in the Ārya Samāj. The slogan of the Ārya Samāj was, "Back to the Vedas." This meant not only an adoption of pre-Buddhist sacrificial religion, but also an elimination of the whole Vedānta philosophy as developed in the *Bhagavad-Gītā* and by Śaṅkara or Rāmānuja. The Ārya Samāj has a very close approach to Islam with its emphasis on one God, one scripture and approval of proselytization. But this did not last long. The clock of progress cannot be set back. The whole development of Hindu religion cannot just be made to stop and retrace its steps. Still Ārya Samāj did remarkable service towards the amelioration of the condition of Hindu women and towards the spread of education and in further breaking the obnoxious caste system.

Thus we had in the eighteenth century a loud proclaiming of social change, often appealing to the Western ideals and patterns unsuited to our genius. But this had no effect on the people because it could not appeal to them and carry their spirit with it. Then in the nineteenth century we had a revival of orthodox conservatism, which was fiercely sentimental and academical. Even this had no far-reaching effect on the people, because it lacked in force and depth and also relevancy to the age.

All this ferment and agitation arose because the Western and Indian cultures were brought face to face and placed in a cauldron. The distinguishing feature of Indian culture is its emphasis on the spiritual and the eternal. This does not mean that Indian culture is unaware of the material and the temporal. In the great days of Aśoka, Harṣa, the Āndhras and Pāṇḍyas and in the days of her colonization — India knew how to integrate the material and spiritual aspects of life. But undue emphasis on the spiritual made the succeeding generations forget the material aspects of her culture. The emphasis of the Buddha on *saṅgha* and the emphasis of *Bhagavad-Gītā* on *karma* were forgotten. This resulted in her foreign subjection, despondency and listlessness. Vitality ebbed out of her and life was sapped out of her. Then came the West. The West due to its exclusive emphasis on the material culture has neglected the spiritual. Totality consists of matter and spirit, the eternal and the momentary. A blind rejection of the West by India would make India lifeless. On the other hand, a complete imitation of the West will make her lose her soul. Either way lies unnecessary danger. If she discards the West and what all it means she will be marooned from the general civilization; and thus the isolation will end in disaster. She should neither embrace the present soulless and atomic culture of the West in full nor loose her ancient moorings.

To deny the superiority of the West, where in fact it is superior, is a folly. But it is equally sheer stupidity to follow the West in everything. Acceptance of all that is of value in the European culture and the absorption of it in the national heritage is the way to success. The spirit of the age is represented by the West. India has much to learn from it — its technology, scientific method and industrial advancement. But the West is also in need of learning much and its advances in technology will give little comfort if it does not learn the deeper lessons of life from India.

11

New Indian Spirit

THE first chapter in the synthesis of Western and Indian cultures began with Vivekānanda. The amazing activity and spiritual personality of Vivekānanda made India to wake from her slumber. To the depressed and demoralized minds of Hindus he came like a stimulating tonic. He travelled not only throughout India, but across the whole earth creating a sensation wherever he went by his sayings and doings. When we think of this *saṁnyāsin* of fiery energy and sincere passion, who wore himself out by ceaseless activity at the early age of 39, we are reminded of the great Śaṅkara. Vivekānanda wanted to combine Western progress with India's spiritual background. "Make a European society with India's religion," he said, "Become an occidental of occidentals in your spirit of equality, freedom, work and energy, and at the same time a Hindu to the very "backbone in religious culture and instincts." Then again, "the fact of our isolation from all the other nations of the world is the cause of our degradation and its only remedy is getting back into the current of the rest of the world. Motion is the sign of life." Immortal and dynamic is the message he gave to India:

> What our country now wants are muscles of iron and nerves of steel, gigantic wills which nothing can resist. . . . Occultism and mysticism — creepy things, there may be great truth in them, but they have nearly destroyed us. Go back to your

> Upaniṣads, the shining, the strengthening, the bright philosophy and part from all these mysterious things, all these weakening things.

According to him, caste was desirable in the early times, but has now become a "monstrous degradation which had crushed masses" and should so be cast away. Intensely patriotic though he was, he was international in outlook and spirit:

> There cannot be any progress without the whole world following in the wake, and it is becoming everyday clearer that the solution of any problem can never be attained on national, racial or narrow grounds.

When extremely orthodox people were trying to narrow and delimit Hinduism almost to insignificance and when so-called radicals were trying to produce a Christian edition of Hinduism, Vivekānanda came and helped towards the survival of Hinduism in the crucial phase. Vivekānanda forces one to believe in what the *Bhagavad-Gītā* declares, "I incarnate for the protection of *dharma* whenever it is in danger."

This new outlook and synthetic spirit which was heralded by Vivekānanda gradually took shape. Unity, synthesis, reconciliation and development through a perfect fusion of old traditions with new values have ever been the characteristics of Hindu culture and religion; and these which were dormant began to work, and produced brilliant personalities, who are the symbols of synthesis and growth. The spirit of the nation, which was curbed for a time by adverse environment, again awoke and rediscovered itself. But this awakening, this Renaissance of a new and synthetic spirit has not yet become the common property of the masses. Unrest and ferment therefore characterize contemporary India. The evolution of the new cultural spirit in India on a mass scale is still in ebullience. Much is expected of this new spirit and culture throughout the world. This is because the second global war has left America in the West and India in the East as the two great powers, with a menacingly uncertain Russia. It remains to be seen what the results of these reactions will be.

Symbolic of this new Indian spirit, but yet linked integrally with its past, stand out three personalities: Aurobindo, Tagore and Gandhi. These three represent the Indian spirit on the supra-mental, mental and vital planes. They have much that is novel in them. But they represent nothing but the dialectical development of the evolution of Hinduism and the "Hindustānī way."

As Romain Rolland says, Aurobindo "is the last of the great *Rsis* who holds in his hands the bow of creative energy." He is one of the greatest contemporary philosophers. His book *The Life Divine* is a classic and represents the complete synthesis of Indian thought. The Śākta-Advaita theory, the *līlā* theory of the Vaiṣṇavas, and the Yoga of the *Bhagavad-Gītā* have been so completely fused together in this work that we have a sublime and novel system of philosophy. Of course, his philosophy has been influenced by the Evolution theory and the systems of European thought. We have to remember the fact that not only has he drunk deep at the living founts of Hinduism, but has delved deep into the European culture and has incorporated the best in the thought-systems of both into his own. This was possible because he combines with his vast erudition in Sanskrit, Greek and English, a daring and penetrating metaphysical insight. Francis Young-husband was not wrong when he characterized Aurobindo's *The Life Divine* as the most significant work of this century. But the other and far significant fact is that he is no mere metaphysician. He has not only scaled and ascended the heights of intellect, but has soared far into the supra-mental regions and has there seen the Divine face to face. No wonder he speaks with a strange force and in a new way. As Tagore has said, anybody who has seen him knows that Aurobindo has found what he was searching for. "He has the word, *mantra*, and the world waits to hear it."

Tagore is a poet (*kavi*) not in the sense that he is a versifier but in the sense that he is the *krānti-darśī*. As a child he was brought up in the most exquisite surroundings of nature — in the Himalaya mountains and in the Gangetic plains. He was not educated in any stereotyped school or college. Nature and select tutors, appointed by his father, were his teachers. Quite early in life he burst forth into the most beautiful songs. Later when the *Gītāñjalī* and *Gora* appeared, the flood gates of Sarasvatī, goddess of knowledge, were thrown open. The *Gītāñjalī* is a collection of ripping poems. They are like the fresh voices of the dawn. They suggest more than they say and seek more than they find. Tagore represents the Hindu outlook which accepts life in full and goes through it with song and dance. Tagore's poems tell us that the world is not made for man. Neither do they preach the pessimistic doctrine — encouraged by H.G. Wells in his later years — that man is only an accident of the vast forces working in the Universe and as such human life has neither a purpose nor a goal. Man, Tagore's poems tell us, is an essential phase in the purposive working out of the spirit. Man reaches his full stature only as he realizes the dignity and worth of life that is not human. Tagore's poems are the torrential outpourings of the earnest yearnings of the human soul. When I read his poems, I am reminded of the Bhāgīrathī flowing down the Himalayas or the Vedic poets singing with the spontaneous joy born of their experience of beauty. He has exerted tremendous influence over the mind of India. All the modern languages of India have been moulded by his writings. No contemporary has worked so much towards bringing the ideals of the East and the West together. Internationalist though in outlook, in his enthusiasm for the whole world, he has not forgotten either his tradition or culture. His mind was thoroughly saturated with the Upaniṣadic wisdom. His *Sādhanā* is the best exposition of the Upaniṣadic teaching. But his greatest achievement is the Viśvabhāratī. His powerful personality has made it a focus of Indian culture. He has suffused it with the spirit of Nalandā, Takṣaśilā and Amarāvatī.

If Aurobindo represents the spiritualistic tradition of India and Tagore its artistic and poetic, Gandhi represents its ceaseless activistic and vital tradition.

"What, O Lord, makes a God out of man?" the disciple asks. "Verily it is fearlessness and purity of being," (*abhayam satva saṁśuddhihī*) declares the *Bhagavad-Gītā*. If that be what makes one a *devatā*, then Gandhi is one. He is fearless to the core. The essence of his teaching is also fearlessness and truth. According to our old books the greatest boon is said to be the attainment of fearlessness. "The dominant impulse in India under British rule was that of fear, pervasive, oppressing, strangling fear of the army, the police, the widespread secret service, fear of the official class; fear of laws meant to suppress and of prison; fear of the landlord's agent; fear of the moneylender, fear of unemployment and starvation which were always on the threshold." Then Gandhi came and gave his *abhaya mantra*. As if at the touch of the magician's wand the country awakened and chanted this new *mantra* of fearlessness. "So, suddenly as it were that black pall of fear was lifted from the people's shoulders, not wholly of course, but to an amazing degree." Gandhi, besides this is a personification of truth and sincerity. Whatever advice he gives, he applies to himself. He is one of those who not only preach but act. He is not swerved by the greatest difficulties, neither is he daunted by the biggest obstacles. He never loses his integrity in prosperity or adversity. He is always complete like the Zero, to which another Zero added or subtracted from makes no difference. He seems to be growing in stature even when he is failing. He is like the *pūrṇatā* of the Upaniṣads or the *śūnyatā* of Nāgārjuna, which can neither be replenished nor depleted. Gandhi's conception of non-violence and truth can directly be traced back to the *Bhagavad-Gītā* and to the Buddha's teaching. But Christianity and Tolstoy have influenced him enormously. *Satya* and *ahiṁsā* are known to Indians from distant ages. But Gandhi's contribution lies in applying these ideals towards bringing a political revolution. He has taught the oppressed and the down-trodden not only to be fearless and harmless, but also has shown them how to shake away the shackles of mental and physical bondage. When we become the votaries of truth and the truth alone we cannot follow the external imposition foreign to our being. "I decline to be a slave," he has said, "to precedents or practice." How profound sincerity can bring about a spiritual reconstruction in man has been shown in his lectures. The history of the struggle for freedom in India for the last thirty years shows how effective *ahiṁsā* can be, when it is applied to politics. Gandhi's application of *ahiṁsā* to political life constitutes an epoch in human history, just as Hiroshima and atom bomb do form another epoch. But the world has awakened to the significance of the atom bomb and not to the importance of *ahiṁsā*. Probably it may require another Hiroshima to open the mists that clog this world, though Heaven forbid it; and Gandhi's ambition, he said, "is to wipe every tear from every eye." Einstein, greatest among scientists, advocates the same principles of love, non-violence and truth when he says: "The way to a joyful and happy state is through renunciation and self-limitation everywhere."

Thus Aurobindo, Gandhi and Tagore represent the spirit of the new trends in Indian culture. But these have not as yet affected the man in the farm and in the factory. This is so, because culture is something that emerges at the top — among fertile brains with foresight, toleration and catholicity — and then sinks to the bottom. It is like the dew which comes from the clouds and covers the green grassy land, and shines thereon with the lustre of pearls. The common man is always conservative and clings to old dogmas and conventions. It requires many a jolt to shake him out of his complacent lethargy. But one day he has to do it and then he marches on with new-found speed. Aurobindo, Tagore and Gandhi herald the new and greater India.

12

The Hindu Ideal

THE law of evolution is not operative only in the biological sphere. It is evident everywhere. In life, in morals, in custom and in social and religious institutions there has been an evolution. When new modes of environment so require, new forms of life emerge. Similarly when an institution which was sufficing and adequate for one stage in human history becomes inadequate and burdensome in the next stage, it undergoes many adaptations and modifications. No doubt conservatism and orthodoxy raise furious protests but their voices are soon muffled up and silenced. The inexorable tendency of history cannot be stopped by feeble human efforts. It has to fly unimpeded. The same happened with regard to Indian culture and Hinduism. Time has not stood still in India, nor has Hinduism remained unchanged. There has been continuous progress; and progress means process. The religion of the *Ṛgveda* is the emergent from the various views that were obtained in Vedic India. The Upaniṣads are the culminations of the spiritualism embedded in the *Ṛgveda*. Then again, when this free spirit of Hinduism was killed by dialectical controversies, ceremonial sanctity and moral laxity, the Buddha drew the attention of the misguided age to the simplicity of truth, prevalence of law (*dharma*) in the universe and the need for social reconstruction (*saṅgha*). At the same time when metaphysics was being misinterpreted and an unnecessary retirement from life was being advocated, the *Bhagavad-Gītā* called upon people to look upon the world as the manifestation and not the negation of the Divine and to convert life into a sacrifice unto the Divine. Then came Nāgārjuna and purged the unwholesome ascetic tendencies of corrupted Buddhism, summoned people to the worship of the Buddha and made Buddhism the Great-way and the Broadway (Mahāyāna) to salvation. Years before this, Vyāsa the author-editor of the *Mahābhārata* knitted the heterogeneous cults and systems of thought into a well-knit fabric of spiritual thought, Hinduism. When in course of time, this spirit was lost, Śaṅkara came and restored the lost unity into the fighting creeds and warring principalities. Under the influences of Islam, the *bhakti* schools of Bengal and Maharashtra arose. They gave rise to the beautiful theory of *līlā*. Kabīr, Nānak and Akbar endeavoured to construct a unified religion through a fusion of Islam and Hinduism, but this did not succeed. Then came the British and this stimulated revivalist and reformist movements within Hinduism. The forceful personality and preaching of Vivekānanda stopped this disintegration, and put an end to the discords in Hinduism. The impact of the Western ideas created the necessity to approach the old problems in a new way and restate the old truth. Aurobindo, Tagore and Gandhi have endeavoured to do this. But their outlook and synthetic spirit have not yet permeated the masses. That is why India is in the ferment and Hinduism is in the cauldron.

Hinduism is in one of its crucial evolutionary phases. Much that is unnecessary — many a useless shell and many a burdensome form — has to be purged away. But there is no need to give up the basic principles of Hinduism. They have only to be restated with reference to the needs of the times (*yuga dharma*) and demands of the society. It is yet to be seen of what type this rejuvenated culture and religion will be. But we need to have neither qualms nor misgivings, because evolution always works for the better, from the partial to the complete, from darkness unto light, and from decay unto life. *Asato mā sad gamaya, tamaso mā jyotir gamaya, mṛtyor mā amṛtam gamaya.* This has always been the Hindu ideal.

Part III
The Advaitic Vision

Hinduism is a vast and complex thing, not so much a religion as a great diversified and yet subtly unified mass of spiritual thought, realization and aspiration.

— Sri Aurobindo

1

Self-Consciousness
Svataḥ-Siddha Vijñāna

I MAY be permitted to express the Vedāntic thinking, depending on the classical sources, for it has been laid down that "whenever awake, until death one should utilize his time in Vedāntic-thinking without giving the least scope for desires etc." (*ā suptera mṛteḥ kālam nayed-vedānta-cintayā; dadhyānnā-vasaram kañcit-kāmadīnām manāgapi.*)

Vedāntic thinking is what is in accordance with the Upaniṣads. What do they teach? As Bhagavatpāda Śaṅkara has said, "the definite conclusion of all the Upaniṣads is that the supreme good results from the perfect knowledge of the ground of the universe."

> *jagataśca yanmūlam tat parijñānāt param śreya iti sarvopaniṣadam niścitorthaḥ* ।
>
> — *Praśna Upaniṣad Bhāṣya*, 6.1

As he added, "the definite conclusion of the entire Vedānta is that the own self of every knower is *Brahman*."

> *sarvasya hi veditaḥ svātmā brahmeti sarva vedāntānām niścitorthaḥ* ।
>
> — *Kena Upaniṣad Bhāṣya*, 2.1

So, "all the Vedāntic discussion is always begun for obtaining the knowledge of the unity of the self."

ātmaikatva-vidyā pratipattaye sarve vedāntā ārabhyante ।
— *Brahma-Sūtra Bhāṣya*, 1.1.1

According to Śaṅkara, when scripture and arguments conjointly engage themselves in revealing the unity of the Self, they are capable of showing it like the *bela* fruit in one's palm.

āgamopapattīhi ātmaikatvaprakāśanāya pravṛtte saknutaḥ; karatalagata bilvamiva darśayitum ।
— *Bṛhadāraṇyaka Upaniṣad Bhāṣya*, 3.1.1

As Appayya Dīkṣita pointed out, "the teachers of Vedānta have displayed many styles for establishing the oneness of the Self."

ātmaikyasiddau . . . śaraṇyo nānāvidhā darśitāḥ ।
— *Siddhāntaleśa Saṁgraha*

In this section I propose to follow mainly Śrī Harṣa, one of our greatest dialecticians and poets, a householder who was a *jitendriya* and a respected courtier who used to enjoy the bliss of *Brahman* in *samādhi.*

When there is knowledge (*vijñāna*) no one who has it doubts that he has it or has the valid or the invalid notion that he does not know. The very absence of these latter notions proves the validity of the knowledge one has. Therefore it may be concluded that self-awareness establishes for everyone the nature of the knowledge one has: *sarvajanasvātma samvedana siddhamevāsya bodhasya svarūpam.* What is its nature? It is self-luminous (*sva-prakāśa*) and proved by itself (*svata eva siddha-svarūpa*).[1] What is self-proved for all cannot be denied, and is moreover, confirmed by the presumption (*arthāpatti*) that the validity of knowledge or experience (*anubhava*) cannot be

1. Śrī Harṣa, *Khaṇḍanakhaṇḍakhādya*, p. 44.

established in any other way. By accepting the self-luminosity of knowledge there will be no epistemological defects like infinite regress (*anavasthā*) and non-relation (*asambhava*). The important point is that as self-luminosity alone can be self-proved or self-evident, no attribute can be included in it. So it cannot be indeed spoken of as it has no attribute: *ata eva . . . vāgvyavahāraviṣayatvam.* How is it then spoken of as self-luminous? Only by imposing on it attributes which it does not have and speaking of it in a figurative way. As it is not limited in any way by space, time or any specific characteristic, it is secondarily or indirectly spoken of as "eternal," "all-pervading," "self of all" and "non-dual." Everything said about it is *upacaritam.* The acceptance of such usage implies nothing but the absence of any limitation. Such an absence or negation may be either conceived as nothing different from the place where it resides, or like the mutual negation which is nothing different from the things between which it holds. On the other hand, the negation implied in "non-duality" cannot be objected to, although its counter-positive (*pratiyogin*), viz. duality, has absolutely no existence, just as the negation of an object of erroneous cognition (e.g. of shell-silver).[2]

Śruti is a valid means of knowing, as it reveals *vijñāna* (consciousness), having it as its purport (*tātparya*) by indicating it indirectly or secondarily (*tadetattu śrutyā pramāṇenopa lakṣaṇanyāya tātparyataḥ prakāśyate*). Really *vijñāna* is not involved in the relationship of a denoting word and a denoted thing (*paramārthatobhidhānābhidheya bhāva-viraha*). Yet, in the state of nescience it may be said that Śruti is a valid means of knowledge by having *vijñāna* as its purport. In fact,

2. Ibid., pp. 53-4.

consciousness is established by itself, i.e. it is self proved: *vastutastu svātma siddhameva cidrūpam.*[3] Śaṅkara Miśra explains that when Śruti says, "*Brahman* is eternal, consciousness and bliss" each one of these words having acquired their capacities in the nescient sense, on the strength of their being uttered together and on the strength of purport, make *Brahman* known in the state of nescience. This-constitutes the validity of Śruti:

> *nitya vijñānānanda padairavidyake evārthe pratyekam gṛhītaśaktibhiḥ sambhūyocchāraṇabalāt tātparya balacchavidyādaśāyām brahma bodhyatā iti tatra śrutīnām prāmāṇya mityārthaḥ*

All this discussion becomes necessary only for the sake of making the followers of other philosophical schools comprehend self-luminosity, while for the Advaitins *vijñāna* is self-established on the strength of self-awareness alone.

> *asmābhisṭtu saṁvedanābalādeva svatasiddha rūpam vijñānamāstīyate*[4]

The Advaitins contend that all this universe other than *vijñāna* is neither "real" nor "unreal" in the sense these terms are understood. It is not real if a thing is considered real in case it is definable, for all definitions are defective (*anupapannāni*). It is not unreal, for if it were so it would destroy the entire empirical activity of the thinking men of the world.[5] All things are "indefinable" does not mean that "in-definability" is definable or that it exists; it also is included in the word "all." If definability is considered to be the proof of reality, as it can be shown that no definition stands logical scrutiny, all things are indefinable, hence not real. Indefinability

3. Ibid., p. 55.
4. Ibid., p. 67.
5. Ibid., p. 68.

of the world is thus the result of this position. It is not a thesis of the Advaitins who disengage themselves from maintaining the reality or unreality of the entire phenomenal world taking their stand solely on the absolutely real *Brahman*, of the nature of consciousness which is self-established. Thus their purpose is accomplished and they are happy.

> *vayam sarvaprapañcasattvāsatva vyavasthāpana nivṛttaḥ svataḥ, siddha cidātmani brahmatattve bharamavalambhya caritārdhaḥ sukhamāsmahe* ।[6]

The conclusion is that the world of difference is indefinable and *Brahman* alone is absolutely real and without a second.[7] Moreover, as Vimuktātman pointed out, while the world is indefinable, it is not unspeakable (*na avācya*).

The question "what is the proof of Advaita?" is impossible to be asked without admitting Advaita. If one has no conception of Advaita, a proof of it cannot be asked. If one has, it must be either valid or invalid knowledge. In the former case the basis of that conception is the proof, and in the latter case it is self-contradictory to ask for the proof of a baseless conception. But granting the question to be somehow legitimate, the Advaitin answers that Śruti alone is the means of valid knowledge for Advaita.[8] According to Advaitic epistemology,

(1) Śruti is an independent means of valid knowledge.
(2) it makes coherent existential statements which are not contradicted by other means of valid knowledge, and
(3) all knowledge has inherent validity. Further, the validity of the perception of difference can be refuted,

---

6. Ibid., p. 72.
7. Ibid., p. 75.
8. *śrutirevādvaite pramāṇam* — Ibid., pp. 76-78.

and the impossibility of inference, etc. to refute Advaita can be shown.

Moreover, the very concept of difference is untenable. It cannot be shown to be either the very nature of an object, or its distinct quality. In the former case, for its perception there should be no need for its counter-positive. In the latter case, because of the same difficulty, it cannot be different.[9] Thus even empirical difference is denied. As Śrī Harṣa says, without cognition of non-difference there cannot be cognition of difference; so the first point only must be valid, as it is basic *upajīvya*.[10] The Advaitin however does not admit the complete unreality of difference, but only its absolute reality. He accepts its presence for nescience, i.e. its being the object of wrong cognition and it is that only which is useful for cause-effect relationship:

na vayam bhedasya sarvayaivāsatvamabhyupagacchamaḥ;
kim nāma, pāramārdhika sattvam ।[11]

Lastly, it must be noted that Advaita, though known through means of valid knowledge, is not different from self-conscious *vijñāna*. The absolutely real Advaitic knowledge is not really generated by Śruti, but is only generated in the state of nescience. Advaita is non-different from *vijñāna*, eternal and self-luminous; that is the ever-present knowledge of *Brahman*. It is the highest truth and it never really arises. It is invalidly conceived as generated by Śruti, but this is not contradicted by the valid conception that it is never generated; and it is the eternal self-luminous Self.[12] As Śaṅkarācārya

9. *koyambhedaḥ? kiṁ svarūpameva bhedinah uta dharmaḥ?* etc., vide: Śrī Harṣa, *Khaṇḍanakhaṇḍakhādya*, p. 103f.

10. Ibid., p. 104.

11. Ibid., p. 118.

12. Ibid., p. 121f.

declared, when there is complete awakening there is non-existence of Śruti also.[13]

Advaitic vision, according to Śrī Harṣa, has immediate and undoubted result.[14] This is the claim of all Advaitins. Sarvajñātman says: In this life itself, the experience born out of Vedāntic sentences bears its fruit by giving liberation.

atraiva janmani bhavedapa vargadāyi; vākyaprasū-ātamānubhūti phalā vasānam.

— *Saṁkṣepa-Śārīraka*, 3.349

Did not Śaṅkarācārya say, *Brahman*-knowledge culminates in experience? (*anubhavāvasānā brahmavidyā*). Further, according to Śrī Harṣa, the tendencies of Advaita arise from God's grace.[15] While commenting on the *Brahma-Sūtras* (2.3.41), *parāttu tat śruteḥ*, Śaṅkarācārya said the same. Knowledge leading to liberation comes from God's grace.

To sum up, in the state of nescience by accepting the notion of what is designated and what designates, the meaning (i.e. non-duality) of the *śruti-vākya*s (scriptural sentences) is grasped. Then through the harmonization or clarification of them, and by reflecting on them it is experienced in an astonishing way by becoming the absolutely real self-luminous consciousness itself.[16] Sarvajñātman, however, says: "Reflected in the cognition arising from *tarka* also the inner self without a second flashes forth. But it becomes more vivid, immediate, when it becomes reflected at the level of non-dual reason (*buddhi*) generated by Vedāntic sentences."[17]

---

13. *śruterapyabhāvaḥ prabodhe* — *Bṛhadāraṇyaka Upaniṣad Bhāṣya*, 1.1.
14. *advaita dṛṣṭir dṛṣṭārthadapi* — *Ibid*, p. 124.
15. Śrī Harṣa, *Khaṇḍanakhaṇḍakhādya*.
16. Ibid., pp. 124-25.
17. *Saṁkṣepa-Śārīraka*, 3.306.

The following comments may be made about the above presentation. In his commentaries Śaṅkarācārya maintained that no one is ever aware that he is not, but that he is. On the contrary everyone realizes "I am" though regarding the nature of "I" there is no unanimity. On the above position, the implications are drawn out and developed. Self-awareness which is self-proved is undeniable and ineffable. This is *vijñāna* or *Brahman*. Vedāntic sentences indicate its nature further through their purport in a secondary or indirect way. Whatever is not *vijñāna* may be shown to be indefinable, while, it being self-evident and ineffable, Vedānta does not try to prove its existence or nature. But it can demolish any argument or thesis which contradicts the oneness of the Self by reducing it to absurdity. Śruti is the only means for the knowledge of the non-dual self, whose nature is eternal, immutable, indivisible consciousness and bliss. The production of this knowledge by Śruti is, of course, from the standpoint of ignorance; for, indeed, that knowledge is itself *Brahman*, ever-present. Again from an empirical standpoint it is said that this knowledge is God's gift, for the Upaniṣads clearly superimpose Godness on *Brahman* and then insistently deny it.

aiśvarya varṇa namatisphuṭameva kṛtvā
netityavādi bahuśaḥ śrutibhi prayatnāt
— *Saṁkṣhepa Sārīraka*, 1.193

The word of the God (*Īśvara-śruti*) is not a purport (*tātparya*) and standard (*pramāṇa*) a word of truthful teaching, (*satya bodhaka śruti*).[18]

18. Ibid., 3.157-58.

2

Falsity of the World
Jaganmithyātva

THERE is a good deal of common talk about the world being an illusion or false. This should be avoided; and what the Advaita school says should be grasped correctly. It may be remembered that Śaṅkarācārya said "the falsity of the world is because of its being sublimated." (*vaitadyam bādhyamānatvāt.— Brahma-Sūtra-Bhāṣya,* 3.2.4

Sublimation or suppression (*baddha*) must be distinguished from opposition (*virodha*). *Baddha* is, says the author of the Vivaraṇa School, the removal of nescience, along with its visibly present or concealed effect (*ajñānasya svakāryeṇa vartamānena pralīnena vā saha jñānena nivṛttirbādyaḥ*).

Virodha is, explains the *Pañcapādikā,* the incapacity of two things to coexist at the same place and time, or to be identical. The perceptual knowledge of multiplicity is sublimated by the scriptural knowledge of unity; so the phenomenal world is false. It is *mithyā* because it is perceptible, material and limited, like the shell-silver; but it is not absolutely unreal like the hare's horn or the barren woman's son. The real is what is never sublimated. Perceptibility (*dṛśyatva*) is knowability by consciousness reflected in the modification of the internal organ. Consciousness which is self-luminous is imperceptible.

(1) The world lacks the utter absence of absolute reality (always self-luminous) as well as of its absolute unreality (which is nowhere and never perceptible).

(2) A superimposition is what is really never present in its substratum at any time. Where it is seen it is really not. In *Brahman* the world of difference is not. In other words, the absence of the world is always present and is non-different from *Brahman*. Its counter-positive, the world, is empirically real. But, in as much as the world as well as its absence are both perceptible, both are negated. In any case, the perceptible world by its very nature never abides in *Brahman,* the sole substratum of everything. So, the world is *mithyā,* while the absence of *mithyātva* is *Brahman*.

(3) As already indicated, because the world of name and form along with its cause is removable by the knowledge of the Self (the substratum) it is the counter-positive of the absence coinciding with the intuition of the substratum. Hence also it is *mithyā*.

(4) Perceptibility of a thing as existing where it is not makes it out to be false. The world is the counter-positive of the utter absence of itself in its own basis. Therefore it is *mithyā*.

(5) The knowledge of the unity taught by the Upaniṣadic sentences is through a means of valid knowledge which has no defect, while the knowledge of multiplicity is through a means of knowledge which is not free from defects. The former is absolutely real, while the latter is not, but yet perceptible. In other words, what is different from that which is established by a perfect means of knowledge is *mithyā*. The world being such is *mithyā*. In these five ways Madhusūdana

> Sarasvatī sought to establish the *mithyātva* of the world according to the purport of the Upaniṣadic sentences like "Here there is no plurality"; "The knower of the Self goes beyond sorrow." Certainty of the world's falsity, he held, helps one to experience non-duality.

It may be asked, is the falsity of the world false or not? The Advaitins answer thus: In negating the world in *Brahman* perceptibility is the limiting factor (*avacchedaka*) of negation (i.e. all that is perceptible is negated). So, falsity (*mithyātva*), the world and its existence which is seen, are all negated by reason of their perceptibility. Therefore neither the world nor its falsity is absolutely real.

3

Great Upaniṣadic Sentences
Upaniṣad Mahāvākyas

Śaṅkarācārya and his authentic followers do not admit anything except the Upaniṣadic sentences as the means of valid knowledge (*pramāṇa*) regarding *Brahman*, because all other *pramāṇa*s are based on and are concerned with external objects and material things (*prāg viṣaya, bahirartha niṣṭha, jaḍavastu niṣṭha*). They are useful only for showing that Vedāntic truth is not improbable, and for refuting theories and views opposed to Upaniṣadic teaching (*sambhāvanā viparīta bhāvanānirāsa*). There can be no independent positive perceptual evidence or demonstration of Advaita or even of the existence of Īśvara. Speculative logic, inference and presumption are only useful in clarifying, defending and bringing out the implications of Upaniṣadic sentences.

na hi vidhi-kāṇḍe tarkasamaye
vā kenacidadhi gatassarvasyātmā,

— *Brahma-Sūtras Bhāṣya*, 1.1.4

vinā mahā vākyamato na kaścit
pumāṁsamadvaitamavaitijantu

— *Saṁkṣepa Śārīraka*, 3.303

atroccyate na khalu vedaśirāṁsi muktvā
kiñcitpramāṇamiha tattvanivedanāya

— *Saṁkṣepa Śārīraka*, 2.7

vedānta vākyam iha kāraṇam ātma bodhe
hetvantarāṇi paripanthinibarhaṇāni
— *Saṁkṣepa Śārīraka*, 3.341

Even when it is said that the Veda or Śruti or the Upaniṣads are the *pramāṇa* for *Brahma-jñāna*, only the *mahāvākya*s (i.e. the great sentences like "That Thou Art") are meant and not any other contents in these sacred books. The rest are just secondary, subsidiary, or appendices.

śeṣapannavacojata, avāntaravacaḥ, aṅgabhūta ।
— *Saṁkṣepa Śārīraka*, 3.296f

But when the *mahāvākya*s are heard, meditated and contemplated upon by those who have the qualifications and the capacity to do so, the experience, *anubhava*, which results from it, of course, becomes the *pramāṇa* of *Brahman*. *Anubhava* never arises in one who has not done all this in this or a previous life. But as the Itihāsas and Purāṇas elaborate the meaning of the Veda, Śaṅkara admits that even from them *Brahma-jñāna* may be obtained.[1] According to him, "the *Bhagavad-Gītā* is the summary of the essence of the meaning of the entire Veda and when its meaning is known all human ends are achieved."

tad idam gītā śāstram samasta vedārtha sāra saṁgraḥ bhūtam
tadarthe vijñāte samasta puruṣārtha siddhi

Ultimately the source of *Brahma-jñāna* is Śruti, and, to the extent possible, experience, etc. (*anubhavādayopi yathāsambhavaṁ*) are also its sources.

How does one know that one has obtained *sākṣātkāra* (direct, immediate, awareness) of *Brahman*? If an ethical person

1. *Brahma-Sūtras-Bhāṣya*, 1.3.38.

with a pure and subtle mind who has gone through the Vedāntic discipline is convinced that he has it, he must be right. The testimony for *Brahman*-knowing is the feeling within one's own heart: *sva hṛdaya pratyayam brahma vedanam*. How can others know that one has obtained *sākṣātkāra*? The answer is that through a scrutiny of the life of one who claims so and by examining his behaviour. The Upaniṣads at various places[2] and the *Bhagavad-Gītā* (2.55-72; 12.13-20) have described the pattern of the life and behaviour of such a person. Whosoever is seen to conform to it may be considered to be one who has attained the ultimate God.

---

2. *Bṛhadāraṇyaka Upaniṣad*, 4.4.23.

4

Scripture and Empirical Knowledge

Śruti and Pramāṇantara

According to both Mīmāṁsā and Vedānta there is no conflict between empirical knowledge and Śruti. The latter is authoritative only in matters of super-sensual and spiritual. If it contradicts empirical facts it must be understood to be speaking figuratively, allegorically or for the sake of inducing one to follow a particular course of action for one's own good. Śaṅkarācārya has said: A hundred Śruti texts do not become a *pramāṇa* if they say fire is cold or does not give light; for no one can cognize what is opposed to what is seen.

na ca śrutiśatamapi sītogniraprakāśo
veti bruvatprāmāṇyamupaiti
— *Bhagavad-Gītā Bhāṣya*, 18.67

na ca dṛṣṭavirodhaḥ kenacidabhyupagamyate
— *Bṛhadāraṇyaka Upaniṣad Bhāṣya*, 1.4.10

A scripture may incidentally contain some history or science, but one who depends on it for empirical knowledge is as foolish as Bhāradvāja's son Avakṛta who resorted to *tapas* for obtaining knowledge (*vidyā*) and was admonished by Indra thus: "This is not the way to become educated. Why do you ruin yourself? If you want to be educated, go to a teacher and study under him."

amārga eṣa viprarṣe yena tvam yātumicchasi;
kiṁ vidhāte na te vipra gacchādhīhi gurormukhāt
— *Mahābhārata*, Vanaparva, ch. 135

Recently a number of books have appeared which seek to prove that contemporary science supports some form of Eastern philosophy or mysticism, or what is believed to be common to all Eastern thought. Some of these books are by scientists, while others are by propagandists of semi-scientific and semi-mystic ideas. First of all it is not a fact that the fundamental doctrines of all Eastern philosophies are identical, or that all Eastern mystics hold the same truth. Not to speak of the mutual differences between the East Asian, the South Asian and the West Asian philosophies and mysticisms, do Vedānta, Buddhism and Jainism hold identical doctrines and the same truth? When some writers assert that contemporary science confirms Eastern mystical insights or philosophical doctrines, they are deluded and confusing the naïve.

Scientists like M.E. Omelyanovsky have sought to establish that contemporary science supports dialectical materialism.[1] According to Jacques Monod, pure chance, absolutely free, but blind is at the very root of evolution; and I. Prigogine differs from him. In a number of his speeches Abdul Salam declared that the faith of the physicist and a part of Islamic faith are the same. C. Hartshorne, Bhikṣu Nyanaponika, N.P. Jacobson among others, argue that modern science has come very close to Buddhist philosophy. There are any number of natural and social scientists (e.g. Yukawa) who maintain that contemporary natural science and psychology are in harmony with Kegon or Zen Buddhist insights. Then there are Jaina scientists who feel happy that John von Neumann and E.P.

1. Vide his *Dialectics and Modern Physics*, Moscow, 1979.

Winger have stated that a consistent formulation of the Quantum theory requires a reference to consciousness. Long ago E. Schrodinger elated some Vedāntins when he pointed out that Mach, Avenarius and Schuppe came very near to the Upaniṣadic thinking and that particular lines in modern thought converge in the Vedāntic vision. But they ignore the fact that he contemptuously rejected the *Bṛhadāraṇyaka* doctrine that "he who sees in It plurality transmigrates" (*mṛtyossa mṛtyumāpnoti ya iha nāneva paśyati*) as an eschatological conclusion and the doctrine of salvation by knowledge (*jñānamuktihi*) as unjust. The same sort of people felt gratified when Oppenheimer was reminded of the *Bhagavad-Gītā* verse about "the arising in the sky of the shining brilliance of a thousand suns" when he saw what occurred when an atom bomb was burst. Some of them probably thought atomic science proved the *Bhagavad-Gītā* to be true. According to Heisenberg, Oppenheimer and Bohr, certain epistemological implications of contemporary physics appeared to corroborate some of the points Taoists, Buddhists and others taught. Tielhard de Chardin believed science was leading to the Christian truth as understood by himself.

This much, however, may be conceded. The Quantum theory, especially the Copenhagen interpretation of it (which is more or less based on Bohr's *Complementarity Principle*) and the theories of J.S. Bell, H. Stapp and G. Chew, seem to agree on what follows: Reality is not what it appears; common sense ideas are inadequate to describe the findings of subatomic physics. The observer-observed distinction is not a hard and fast objective one. The scientist is a participant, not a detached observer; so his way of looking at things enters into his theories Opposites (e.g. matter and force, existence and non-existence) are complementary. The world is not substantive as usually thought. It is an interconnected issue of events or an implicative order of that which is, an undivided whole. There are no elementary particles or fundamental fields. Nature is to be understood entirely through its self-consistency.

The above are not the only possible conclusions that can be derived from contemporary scientific developments; and all leading scientists do not unanimously accept them. To say that they prove *Avataṁśaka* (Kegon) Buddhism, Advaita Vedānta or Taoism is unjustified. To say that they prove what is common to all of them raises the question: Is there such a common core of these philosophies accepted by most of their authoritative exponents? The answer has to be definitely negative. It is true that science is increasingly finding a unity amidst the diversity of phenomena and forces. Islam, Salām asserts, always believed so. Buddhism, says Anāgārika Govinda, finds a Self-surpassing Oneness amidst diversity. Uddālaka also thought there is a "Single Principle" by knowing which all that is becomes known, for all things are but its modifications. But there is no unanimity about the nature of that unity or principle, the ontological status of diversity, and the relation between the two either among scientists or philosophers. Some say that it is "Matter" others it is a "Person," some that it is "Emptiness," and yet others that it is "Consciousness." Science neither supports nor contradicts these, whatever they may be, whether revelations, intuitions or speculations.

In this matter the standpoint of Śaṅkara's school is clear. Śruti, it maintains, gives knowledge which does not fall within the scope of other *pramāṇa*s, i.e. of empirical knowledge. So empirical knowledge cannot strengthen or reinforce Śruti. It is unique because it does not give knowledge of something known otherwise also. Otherwise it would become weaker or a non-*pramāṇa*. There are Upaniṣadic texts which speak about difference (*bhedaśrutis*) just reiterating what perception conveys. There are Upaniṣadic texts which teach Oneness (*abhedaśrutis*), conveying something unique, what is not known in any other way. So, the latter are more powerful and set aside the former. The Śruti which is not confirmed by other *pramāṇas*, or which does not confirm what other *pramāṇas* make known, is stronger than that which is confirmed by other *pramāṇas* or which just confirms what is made known by other *pramāṇas*. The Śruti which reveals what is unknowable through perception and inference is really authentic. Difference and multiplicity are seen everywhere in the world. The Śruti which propounds them is weak. Non-difference and oneness is nowhere perceived in the world. So the Śruti which propounds it is strong. According to Madhva, that was Śaṅkara's view:

prābalyamāpādayati śrutīnām
mānāntaram naiva budhāgrayāyin!
gatārthatādānạmukhena tāsām
daurbalyasampādakameva kintu!!

— Madhvācārya, *Śaṅkara Digvijaya*, 8.130

It is rash to hold that the Upaniṣads depend on any other *pramāṇas*.

sāpekṣatopaniṣadāṁ yadi sāhasam tat ।

— Sarvajnātman, op. cit., 1.541

Neither contemporary science nor future science, classical Vedānta maintains, can or need confirm the truth that the One Reality of the nature of consciousness and bliss is without a second and that "I am that" and "All this is that." No science is or ever can be opposed to that. This truth has been and can be confirmed in one way only: by one's own experience. Hence it is *svānubhūtyekamān.*[2] Brian Josephson expressed a balanced view when he said that consciousness has not yet been understood and its understanding lies outside the paradigm of physics. Something more about the nature of reality, he added, may be learnt through meditative processes, but its results may not be universally persuasive.

5

Transcendental Knowledge and Secular Activity

Tattva-Jñāna and Laukika-Vyavahāra

THE ethical and socio-political implications of Advaita Vedānta are also important. The *Bhagavad-Gītā* has pointed out that those for whom duality has been destroyed (*chinna dvaidhaḥ*) and have become equal-minded (*sama buddhayaḥ*) will be engaged in the welfare of all beings.[1] The great men who have won peace, says Śaṅkara, work for the world's welfare (*śāntā mahānto lokahitam carantaḥ*). One who knows that his self is the self of all beings[2] realizes that if he harms others he harms himself, whereas if he does well to others, he does well to himself. For such a man there is no enemy, as there is no other. The consequence of the awareness of identity necessarily results in equality. The metaphysics of Advaita can be the foundation only for unselfishness and altruism and is consistent only with an egalitarian society based on social and economic justice and equality and peace. *Chinna dvaidhaḥ* and *sama buddhayaḥ* cannot accept any socio-political system which gives scope for privileges and monopolies or inequality and injustice, based on any kind of difference due to birth, position, wealth

---

1. *Bhagavad-Gītā*, 5.25; 12.4.
2. *sarvabhūtātmābhūtātmā*, — *Bhagavad-Gītā*, 5.7.

or power. *Ṛta* and *dharma* will prevail in a Vedāntic social order. Advaita and *samatva* in thought and deed go together. On the contrary, to maintain that Advaita should remain only an idea (*bhāva*) and not be translated into practice (*kriyā*) is illogical and schizophrenic. Only in a split personality would *darśana* be different from *vartana*, not in an integrated person who has realized *abheda* and *samatva*. We, therefore, rejoice that Śrī Abhinava Vidyātīrtha Mahāswāmi, the greatest living representative of Ādi Śaṅkarācārya, has "urged people to give up traditions based on injustice and dogma, based on blind faith, and follow religion which teaches principles of life." He "exhorted his devotees to keep in mind that they were Indians first and try to break the barriers of casteism."[3]

According to Sureśvara, humility (*amānitva*) and non-hatred (*adveṣatva*) are the instruments (*sādhanās*) for the seeker of *Brahma-jñāna*, whereas they constitute the very nature of a *Brahma-jñānī*. Neither the former who would have no attachment to anything, nor the latter whose actions would be free from the moulding of desire *kāmasaṁkalpavarjitaḥ*[4] would indulge in wanton behaviour (*yatheṣṭācaraṇa*). He who seeks *Brahma-jñāna* as well as he who has it can be only ethical personalities.[5] This disposes of the notion that actions do not bind him; a *Brahma-jñānī* may behave as he likes. Anyone who does so, says Sureśvara, will not be different from a dog.

It is interesting that two eminent direct disciples of Śaṅkara had great regard for the life of a householder.

---

3. Śrī Abhinava Vidyātīrtha Mahāswāmi is the Head of the most important Hindu monastic establishment in the world at Śṛṅgerī, and a profound scholar of Nyāya and Vedānta. His Speech at Nasik, *The Hindu*, May 4, 1982.

4. *Bhagavad-Gītā*, 4.19.

5. *Naiṣkarmyasiddhi*, IV.69, 62-67.

According to Madhva, Sureśvara is reported to have said, "It is the mind which is the cause of bondage or liberation. Whether one is a householder or a *saṁnyāsin*, what is necessary is pure mind."

mano viśuddho gṛhī bhāvedvapyuta maskarī va ।

— *Śaṅkara Digvijaya,* 13.57

The same source attributes the following view to Padmapāda: "the basis of all human ends is the body, which can be sustained by food only. Food is produced only by householders. So all fruits (values) ultimately depend on householders."

sarvam phalam gehapatidrumāśrayam ।

— *Śaṅkara digvijaya,* 14.103

The relation between action and knowledge in Advaita Vedānta has been much discussed by some modern scholars. The classical position on this has been clearly set forth by Vidyāraṇya in his *Pañcadaśī.*

The following is a summary of relevant verses in *Tṛptidīpa* of his *Pañcadaśī*: One who seeking *Brahman* knowledge is practising (*abhyāsa, anusandhāna*) meditation and contemplation (*manana* and *nididhyāsana*) should avoid such activities which disturb the notion "I am *Brahman*" by distracting him and making him forget that truth; but he may do all that is necessary to sustain life as well as whatever does not distract or disturb him much. But one who has firm awareness (*dṛḍha-bodha*) may do anything e.g. study poetry or history, teach logic, engage in agriculture, or rule a kingdom: *tarkam patha yaddha kṛṣi kuru.* While engaged in action according to the *prārabdha-karma* (previous action which has already begun bearing fruit) in order to exhaust the momentum of the latter, the wise men do not suffer the misery of transmigration (*saṁsāra-tāpa*) caused by delusory cognition (*bhrānti-jñāna*), which they have got rid of. But they may feel sorry for themselves because though they have no attachment they are obliged to engage in action as their *prārabdha-karma* has not come to an end. Thus their sorrow is a result of discrimination (*viveka*), while the misery of others is *saṁsāra*. For this reason wise men, due to *prārabdha*, may desire enjoyment, but will not delight in it; and having no desire they will be satisfied with very little enjoyment, while those without discrimination will not be satisfied even with much enjoyment.[6]

The relevant verses in *Dhyānadīpa* of the *Pañcadaśī* may be summarized thus: Secular-activity (*laukika-vyavahāra*) is not opposed to *Brahman*-knowledge; so one who knows the truth, may very well engage himself in it: *tattvavittva virodhitvāllaukikam samyagācaret*. How is the awareness that this world is illusory (*māyāmaya*) and the self is of the nature of consciousness opposed to secular activity? Secular activity does not require that the world be real; it only requires that one is a conscious being (not *jaḍa*) and that means (*sādhanā*s) are available. Mind, speech, body and external objects are the means which have not been rejected or suppressed by a wise man. So, one who has *Brahman*-knowledge and has the means can very well engage himself in secular activity e.g. ruling a kingdom.[7] As a man with *Brahman*-knowledge does not become oblivious of the world, he may happily engage himself in external activity (*pravartatam sukhenayam*); there is no harm. When one has intellectually and emotionally abandoned all attachment and involvement and has pure knowledge, he may or may not perform actions (*karmāni karotu mā karotu*); for his actions have

---

6. *Tṛptidīpa*, 123-132, 143-46.

7. *Dhyānadīpa*, 87-90, 114.

been anyway destroyed by *samādhi*. When a man's mind has no impressions (tendencies = *nirvāsana*), he has no purpose to be gained by actionlessness, action, *samādhi* or *japa*.

naiṣkarmyeṇa na tasyārthastasyārthopi na karmabhiḥ ।[8]

Reverting to equality which I consider as important as identity I would like to draw attention to some of the invaluable sayings of Ādi Śaṅkarācārya on it. We learn from his *magnum opus*, that the true self is devoid of distinctions like brāhmin, kṣatriya, etc. Caste, life-stage, age, situation, etc. are superimposed on it.

apeta brahma kṣatrādi bhedamātma tattvam ।

— *Brahma-Sūtras-Bhāṣya*, 1.1.1

The *Bṛhadāraṇyaka Upaniṣad Bhāṣya* (11.4.5) has a similar passage. His *Ātma-Bodha* teaches: "Just like the differences of taste, colour, etc. in water, caste, name, life-stage, etc. are superimposed on the self due to limiting adjuncts"

nānopādhivasādeva jāti namāśramādayaḥ;
ātmanyāropitāstoye rasavarṇādi bhedavat ॥

His *Maniṣa-Pañcakam* declares that as the same self is in all and as the bodies of all are made up of the same stuff, even a person of the so-called lowest birth is to be considered a *guru* if he has the awareness of his identity with the one consciousness that interpenetrates everything. Śaṅkarācārya's *Daśa-Ślokī* affirms: "For me there are no caste or rules of conduct for caste and life-stages, because of the destruction of the superimposition of "I" and "mine" on the self. So I am the absolutely only one that remains viz. Bliss: *na-varṇa na-*

8. *Dhyānadīpa*, 98, 102-3.

varṇāśramācāra dharmaḥ . . . śivaḥ kevaloham. His *Tattva-Bodha* (47) asserts: "It does not matter whether one dies in Varanasi or in a dog-eater's house. What matters is to have the knowledge of the self, which alone leads to liberation." Has any other religious teacher simultaneously emphasized Identity and Equality with greater force?

Likewise Vidyāraṇya affirmed that the wise man is convinced that due to *māyā* caste, station in life, etc. have been imagined in the body, and not in the self which is of the nature of awareness.

> *varṇāśramādayo dehe māyayā parikalpitāḥ* ।
>
> — *Pañcadaśī, Dhyānadīpa*, 101

Elsewhere he wrote, one who has the notion that the brāhmin-caste (*vipra-jāti*) is a thing different from consciousness suffers from the delusion "I am a brāhmin." The vision of the indivisible All (*sarvakhaṇḍa darśana*) is possible only for one whose perception of caste, etc. has been removed.

I hope everyone who cherishes Advaita will someday be sincerely capable of echoing the rapturous words of the wonderful and extraordinary disciple of Śaṅkarācārya, Hastāmalaka, and practising what it implies: "I am not a man, god or *yakṣa*; nor am I a brāhmin, kṣatriya, vaiśya or śūdra. I am not even a celibate, householder, forest-dweller or renunciant, I am true Awareness itself." *Nija bodha rūpaḥ*.

Index